WEIGHT TRAINING
IN ATHLETICS

WEIGHT

TRAINING

IN

ATHLETICS

JIM MURRAY
Co-director, the Varsity Barbell Club,
   Morrisville, Pa.
Former Managing Editor, *Strength and Health*

PETER V. KARPOVICH, M.D.
Research Professor of Physiology,
   Springfield College

With Sketches by Jim Murray

Prentice-Hall, Inc.

Englewood Cliffs, N. J.

Contents

──────── *Part I* ────────

1 The Rise of Weight Lifting in the
U.S.A. 3

European influence . . . 4

Early North American strongmen . . . 11

The mail-order instructors . . . 12

International rise of U.S. lifters . . . 15

Russians rise as Egyptians fade . . . 18

The "Mr." contests . . . 21

Conditioning value of weight training . . . 23

References . . . 24

v

—————————— *Part II* ——————————

2 The Men in the Sport 29

People in glass houses . . . 30
Are weight lifters dumbbells? . . . 30
Who lifts weights in our country? . . . 31

3 Muscles and Strength 34

How muscles change during training . . . 37
How fast do muscles grow? . . . 37
How much does strength depend on weight? . . . 40
The muscle-bound myth . . . 44
Speed . . . 45
Flexibility . . . 47
You must have a plan to exercise properly . . . 48
How much time does it take? . . . 49
Weight lifting without weights . . . 50

4 Effects of Weight Lifting on the Body   51

Energy used in weight lifting . . . 51
Weight lifting and pulse rate . . . 55
Weight lifting and blood pressure . . . 56
What should the athlete eat? . . . 58
Injuries in weight lifting . . . 64
References . . . 66

Part III

5 Basic Conditioning and Strengthening
     Through Resistance Exercise   .   .   71

*Basic exercises (Warm-up. Curl. Press. Rowing.
Squat. Pullover. Rise-on-toes. Dead lift. Upright rowing. Press on bench. Bent-arm lateral
raise, lying. Lateral raise, standing.) . . . 75*

The abdominal muscles . . . 83

6 Weight Training Variation Exercises   84

For the forearm flexors and wrists . . . 85

For the arm extensors . . . 86

For the shoulders (deltoid muscles) . . . 87

For the chest . . . 88

For the upper back . . . 89

For the lower back and hips . . . 90

For the thighs (extensors) . . . 91

For the thighs (flexors) . . . 92

For the trunk . . . 93

For the calves . . . 94

For the neck . . . 94

Use of variation exercises . . . 95

A "keep fit" routine . . . 100

References . . . 100

—————— *Part IV* ——————

7 For the Instructor and Coach . . . 103

Equipment for weight training . . . 104

Use of weight training exercises in groups . . . 105

Points for emphasis by instructors . . . 107

Grading a weight training class . . . 109

Supine press on bench . . . 111

Curl with barbell . . . 112

Full knee bend . . . 112

Dead weight lift . . . 112

Sit-up with weight . . . 112

8 Resistance Exercises for Football
Players 114

9 Resistance Exercises for Basketball
Players 122

10 Resistance Exercises for Baseball
Players 126

11 Resistance Exercises for Track and
Field 130

12 Weight Training for the "Minor"
Sports 139

For wrestlers . . . 139
For swimmers . . . 141
For boxers . . . 144
For oarsmen . . . 146
For tennis players . . . 147
For golfers . . . 147
For fencers . . . 149
References . . . 153

─────────────── *Part V* ───────────────

13 Weight Lifting in Competition . . 157

The two-arms press . . . 161
The two-arms snatch . . . 173
The two-arms clean and jerk . . . 186
Building power and strength . . . 198
Arranging training schedules . . . 201
Selecting lifts in competition . . . 203
References . . . 208

Index 209

To the Reader

THIS book has a dual purpose: first, to supply practical directions for weight training that can be successfully applied to competitive weight lifting and body building or that can be used as an aid in conditioning for various sports.

And, secondly, our purpose has been to give a glimpse into the physiological and medical aspects of weight training.

Although this book represents a cooperative effort, each author has had a large degree of independence in writing his part of the book.

JIM MURRAY
PETER V. KARPOVICH, M.D.

Part I

Part II

Chapter 1

The Rise of Weight Lifting
in the U.S.A.

THE great Greek wrestler, Milo of Croton, who won fame in ancient Olympic Games, is the first weight lifter of note in recorded history. The story often has been told of how young Milo, to strengthen himself for all-out wrestling contests that frequently ended in death for the vanquished, practiced lifting a young bull and walking with it on his shoulders daily as it grew to its full size.

Milo's principle of gradual progression from a relatively light weight to a heavy poundage is the same one followed today to develop strength and improve physical condition by exercising

3

with adjustable barbells and dumbbells. Incidentally, according to ancient Greek stories of the Olympic Games, Milo developed tremendous strength that served him in good stead as he became the athletic hero of his day. Competing in an era when bones were broken, ears torn off, and eyes gouged, Milo's long reign as a champion attested to the value of his strength-building routine.

European influence

Although it has only recently begun to gain favorable recognition in the United States, weight lifting in various forms is one of the most ancient of physical activites. Other "basic sports" are competition in running, jumping, throwing, swimming, and wrestling. These activities are the ones that develop physical characteristics always considered desirable through necessity: strength, speed, agility, and hardiness.

Today, the evolution of modern society makes it much less necessary for Man to be strong, fast, agile, and rugged. Machines do his work and provide transportation, and social behavior makes ruggedness actually unnecessary. There seems, however, to be an inherent instinct in Man that makes his desire to have the old-time qualities once so vital to his very survival.

Thus we have systems of exercise and competitive athletic games that enable us to give vent to an instinctive urge to excel physically as well as intellectually and economically. And it is well that we do, for it has been learned that physical fitness proves an asset to mental alertness.

In modern America, to a greater degree than in the rest of the world, it has become fashionable to believe that an intrepid little fellow without much muscle can always win over the big husky brute in tests of physical ability, through greater mobility and skill. Popular fiction and entertainment, such as the motion pictures, have contributed to this belief by glorifying the slender, handsome hero who easily mops up a roomful of "baddies"—all large, beefy, and fortunately equipped with two left feet—without even mussing his hair. American sports evolution has kept pace with and added to this illusion, stressing competition with emphasis on skill, such as basketball and baseball, with rules avoiding violence or any circumstance in which sheer strength can become a primary asset.

This is also true of the United States' third major sport, football, to a certain extent. But in football, body contact is still of the essence and on the football field the fiction is ended when we see the advantage possessed by skilled players who have unusual strength and size. An activity in which strength can be even more advantageous, wrestling, has never gained great popularity as a spectator sport in America.

Fashionable beliefs to the contrary, coaches and competing athletes know that a skilled man with strength always has an advantage over a man who depends on skill alone. In addition, it is easier for a strong man to develop endurance and learn to move his body effectively because his muscles have the ability to carry him through the necessary movements.

In European and Asiatic countries, strength has always come in for as great a share of admiration as other physical attributes. It was in Germany and other Middle European countries that weight lifting, as we know it today, got its start. During the 19th century, untold numbers of professional strongmen lifted their barbells and performed spectacular stunts with carnivals and on vaudeville stages. Most of them got their starts in amateur clubs, often in the back rooms of taverns where vigorous young men met to wrestle, box, and lift weights. The weights lifted in early days of the sport were solid and clumsy. Iron globes were cast with iron or steel connecting bars, and other weights were cast as single globes or blocks with projecting handles. These were not unlike the 35-pound and 56-pound weights thrown in track and field competition today, except that the handles were not flexible.

A man had to be strong even to make a start as a weight

lifter when barbells were not adjustable. Therefore it was not until the development of the adjustable barbell that weights came into use as a strengthener of the person below par physically.

Because so many of the old athletic clubs were conveniently located near refreshment, strength greats of the last century were often huge men, naturally big and strong enough to handle the clumsy weights. They added to their size by developing, literally, "beer bellies" as well as big muscles.

Among those most famed for brute strength from the group of massive Germans who alternately lifted steins and dumbbells were Josef Steinbach and Karl Swoboda. Like their contemporaries, they ranged from 250 to 300 pounds in body weight and had large waistlines to match their massive arms and legs. Steinbach placed most of his weight lifting emphasis on the handling of heavy, short-handled dumbbells and was able to set a mark of 70 kilos (154 pounds) in each hand, pressing the weights overhead simultaneously. To press a 308-pound barbell would have been a great feat in Steinbach's day, but it is even more difficult to handle two ponderous individual weights in this manner. It was not until the advent in 1953 and 1954 of Doug Hepburn and Paul Anderson, faster-moving throwbacks to the 19th century's style of heavyweight, that anyone even threatened to exceed Steinbach's mark.

Swoboda, partially because his generous waistline impeded the upward progress of barbells from the floor to his chest and partially because he just liked to lift heavy weights overhead, gained fame from shoving heavy barbells up to locked arms. There was little interest in the quick lifts of modern competition. Contests were arranged according to the specialties of the contestants, so lifters tried to gain supremacy in pet feats. With the assistance of other lifters who handed him the barbell at chest height, Swoboda jerked 200 kilos—440 pounds—overhead. This is another record that was unchallenged until recent years, when 300-pound Doug Hepburn shoved 490 pounds up from the shoulders. Another Swoboda specialty, however, has been bettered by a much smaller man, 225-pound Norbert Scheman-sky, Olympic champion and Sullivan award nominee. Swoboda had lifted 409 pounds from the floor to arms' length overhead in what is called the "continental" style, allowing an unlimited number of movements to the chest. Schemansky, strong and more agile than Swoboda, lifted 440 pounds first to his belt, then to his chest, and then jerked the barbell overhead. Sche-mansky made his 200-kilo lift at Vienna in 1953, where old weight lifters said now they had "seen everything."

Since Schemansky lifted his 440, however, the record for continental style lifting has returned to the giants, with the modern colossus Paul Anderson elevating 457 pounds. This lift, performed during a tour of the Far East by a group of American AAU athletes, is the heaviest weight ever lifted overhead from the floor without assistance. Anderson weighed approximately 340 pounds when he made the lift.

During the early 1900's, another great German professional strongman held forth on the Continent and in tours of South Africa and England. Unfortunately, the lifts which give Herman Goerner his greatest claim to fame seem shrouded in mystery and there is some question as to their authenticity. Goerner was a physical giant; 72½ inches tall, with a reach (fingertip to fingertip) of 78¼ inches. At the age of 43, when he weighed 290 pounds, Goerner's measurements included 19½-inch neck, 50½-inch chest, 45¼-inch waist, 19-inch flexed right arm, 9-inch wrist, 27-inch thigh, and 18-inch calf. He did his best lift-ing a few years earlier, weighing 264 pounds, and is reputed to have lifted 390 pounds overhead in two movements (clean and jerk). It has also been reported that Goerner straightened up and raised a 793¾-pound barbell from the floor to a position across his thighs (dead weight lift), and that he shouldered a barbell weighing 442¼ pounds in two movements (one to waist and another to chest, stopping at the belt). If all the lifts credited to Goerner are accurate, he was one of the strongest men of all time.

It is possible that Goerner may have succeeded with the lifts credited to him, for several men have exceeded his best clean and jerk. Norbert Schemansky, a smaller man, has bettered his two-movement lift to the shoulders by raising 450 pounds, which was not his limit. (Schemansky was attempting a complete continental and jerk, and got the weight to his chest with comparative ease, failing to hold it overhead.) No one has beaten Goerner's dead lift, therefore this feat of basic strength, if authentic, ranks Goerner among the foremost of the all-time great strongmen.

Another of the great German professional strongmen, perhaps the greatest, was Arthur (Hennig) Saxon, who also did his best lifting during the early nineteen hundreds. Not a huge man by any means, the 69½-inch Saxon never weighed more than 210 pounds; nevertheless, he has the distinction of having lifted more weight overhead under control than anyone except Paul Anderson. The method by which Saxon lifted 448 pounds unassisted required not only great all-around strength, but also coordination, balance, stamina, and great determination. He began by shouldering with two hands, a 336-pound barbell, which he then held at the right shoulder with his right hand centered on the bar. Leaning to his left and supporting his right upper arm along his body, he lowered himself away from the weight until the arm was nearly straight and then locked out the 336-pound weight by arm strength. While in the low position, leaning to the side, he reached down and grasped a 112-pound kettlebell (similar to a throwing weight, but with a short, rigid handle) which he pulled up as he straightened and then pushed up alongside the heavier weight. (*See* Figure 1.) No one has ever approached Saxon's record in the same style used by the great German professional when he made what was termed a "two-hands anyhow" in the year 1905.

Saxon was noted for his proficiency in many other lifts, notably the first portion of the anyhow, called the "bent press." In this one-handed lift he unofficially lifted an incredible 370 pounds! Another of Saxon's amazing feats was to toss a 315-pound barbell from one hand to the other, overhead, after bent pressing the weight. Included in his stage show were the lifting of a loaded platform weighing 3500 pounds on his back (pushing with arms and legs to clear platform of supports) and a support of 3200 pounds on straight legs in a supine position.

Figure 1. Saxon's famous unassisted overhead lift.

During the years Saxon and his brothers held forth with their strongman trio act, another great weight lifter was winning world renown on the wrestling mat. George Hackenschmidt began his athletic career as a lifter, winning amateur championships, and was one of the first great athletes to demonstrate that strength so developed could be used to good advantage in another sport. At his best using the Greco-Roman style, Hackenschmidt, in his prime, is still rated by many experts as having been the greatest wrestler of the century. Hackenschmidt used weight lifting exercises throughout his career, but as a young man set such records as a world mark in the one-hand snatch (a lift overhead in a single, unbroken motion from the floor) of 197½ pounds during the year 1898. As an impromptu stunt,

Hackenschmidt once assumed the wrestler's bridge position, then reached back and pulled over a 311-pound barbell to his chest. Still in the bridge, he pressed the weight up to locked arms twice. This feat has never been equalled. One of Hackenschmidt's training innovations was to kneel on hands and knees, while supporting a sack weighing six hundredweight, with a 230-pound wrestler seated on the sack. This stunt made him difficult to "break down" if an opponent was able to get behind him on the mat.

A French lifter, who was at his best twenty years after the era of Saxon, Swoboda, Steinbach, and Hackenschmidt, did much to put emphasis on speed in weight lifting. This was Charles Rigoulot, Olympic Games lightheavyweight champion in 1924. Rigoulot was far from his best strength at that time, but made a one-hand snatch with 192 pounds. Note the close approach to Hackenschmidt's record made twenty-six years earlier. In 1930 Rigoulot improved on the one-hand snatch record with a lift that is unapproached, variously reported at 253½ and 256½ pounds. The snatch lift, performed with a fast, high pull and quick dropping under the weight, enabled the French heavyweight to employ his agility to advantage. At a height of 68 inches, Rigoulot had amazing speed for a man weighing 230 pounds. It was his power, strength with speed, that made him the first man to lift over 400 pounds in the clean and jerk. Lifting as a professional, with a specially designed barbell that would not be acceptable in standard amateur contests, Rigoulot lifted his 402 pounds—and it was nearly twenty years before another lifter was able to match the feat!

Many of the great European professionals toured the United States, helping to foster interest in weight lifting and feats of strength. The Saxons toured America and made a profound impression on youngsters like Harry Paschall, later a national champion lifter and record-holder, who became one of the most popular writers in the field after retiring from competition. Paschall, after seeing great strongmen and lifters in action over a period of more than forty years, still ranks Saxon the greatest of all time.

A man who could not begin to match Saxon as a strongman, however, probably had more influence than any other in making America muscle conscious. This man, Eugene Sandow, might not have done so but for the promotion arranged by his famous manager, Florenz Ziegfeld. While Sandow trailed Saxon by 100 pounds in the bent press, his handsome appearance and showmanship made him the inspiration of thousands.

Early North American strongmen

It was a good thing for weight lifting that the European Sandow's exhibitions in America showed a trim, well-proportioned man could be strong, and that in gaining strength by lifting weights, he retained his Greek-godlike physique. One of the greatest native North American strongmen of all time, a contemporary of Sandow, Louis Cyr, had convinced many casual observers that his ponderous size was due to the fact that he lifted weights, rather than to a combination of body type and appetite. Cyr, a 69-inch Canadian who weighed approximately 300 pounds, performed some astounding strength feats, just prior to the turn of the century, to gain fame as "the strongest man who ever lived." Primarily interested in stunts in which he lifted heavy platforms with a number of persons standing on them, Cyr was able to raise two tons clear of supports by pushing upward with arms and legs while bracing his back against the underside of a platform. To demonstrate the great strength of his shoulders, Cyr held out, at straight arms to the sides, a 94-pound dumbbell in his right hand and an 88-pound dumbbell in his left. Although not interested in the lifts now standardized for competition, Cyr was far ahead of his time in pressing 300 pounds overhead without special training on the lift. Cyr was also said to have performed a one-hand snatch (with both left and right arm) of a solid, non-revolving barbell, weighing 188½ pounds, that had a handle 1½ inches in diameter! Not only was the weight a near-record poundage at the time, but a solid bell is a cumbersome object even with a normal-sized handle (1⅒ inches diameter). With a thick handle, the grip strength involved in pulling the weight up quickly from the floor makes the feat one of the greatest of all time. Another great grip (and all-around) feat credited to Cyr is a one-hand dead weight lift of 525 pounds on a 1½ -inch bar, one more stunt of timeless merit even on a standard barbell.

The United States also produced its share of professional strongmen. One was Warren Lincoln Travis, who held forth at Coney Island with sensational feats. A great boost to the weight lifters of his day was Henry Steinborn, rugged professional wrestler who settled in the U.S. after World War I. Steinborn showed by his personal example that 300 pounds was just another weight in the clean and jerk, not an impassable barrier. Seeing him in action enabled American lifters to "set their sights higher." Steinborn, incidentally, performed one of the truly great strength feats of all time when he performed a full knee bend with 550 pounds *unassisted*. He up-ended the barbell and then squatted quickly to catch the weight across the shoulders, from which position he rose by straightening his powerful legs.

The mail-order instructors

With the inspiration of the leading professionals, including many worthy performers not mentioned here, weight training also received a great boost from the thinkers and organizers, the men who sold weights and instruction by mail order.

One of the first instructors was Theodore Siebert, who developed in Germany a training routine that was not basically different from the exercises used today. France also had its "train-you-by-mail" instructor in Edmund Desbonnet. Sandow took a brief fling at selling the body building "secrets" of his own success, but did not present the heavy barbell and dumbbell routines he actually practiced. Instead he praised the merits of a light dumbbell course, little more advanced than calisthenics, for strength-building.

In the United States, the first instructor to bring sound weight training methods to a mass audience was Alan Calvert, who established the Milo Barbell Company in 1903. Calvert sold a course of weight training that could still be followed today with good results. His first barbells had hollow globes on the ends and could be made progressively heavier by pouring shot into the ends. Later he began using plates of different weights, similar to those used to grade the resistance of barbells today. Calvert was a truly inspirational writer in his book *Super Strength,* now a collector's item, and in a small magazine he published called *Strength.* His courses were divided into three stages: a basic routine of a dozen exercises; a more advanced routine, including heavier leg work and teaching lifts in vogue, such as the one-arm bent press; and a third course, which taught the strongman stunts used by stage performers. Calvert improved on the ideas of continental instructors Siebert and Desbonnet by recognizing the need for a rebuilding period between exercising sessions. He taught that the body's strength and muscle size would develop more quickly if the days of exercise were separated by days in which no exercise was practiced. Later the Milo Barbell Company and *Strength* magazine were headed by Mark Berry, who was also official coach of the 1936 Olympic team. A victim of the same financial troubles that plagued the rest of the country, the original Milo company was bought by Bob Hoffman in 1934. Two years earlier Hoffman had founded the York Barbell Company.

Hoffman's start as a weight training mail-order instructor and manufacturer resulted from personal interest in athletics. Weighing 180 pounds at more than 74 inches in height, Hoffman was a salesman for oil burners produced in York, Pa. He was also active in local YMCA sports and gained fame for his ability in canoe racing. Interested in physical activity of all kinds, Hoffman became an enthusiastic weight lifter when he learned of this type of exercise. He found that he gained in size and strength from weight training as he never had from his other athletic participation. He became a full-fledged heavyweight of 230 pounds, competing in weight lifting contests as a member of the York Oil Burner Athletic Club. Hoffman also continued his interest in YMCA competition in track and field and events, as well as canoeing and rowing. Finding that his performance improved as he gained size and strength, he became the first man to widely publicize his belief—*weight training could help athletes in other sports* of their choice.

In 1932 Hoffman began publication of *Strength and Health* magazine. He extolled the merits of weight training as an exercise and weight lifting as a sport, and, of course, used the magazine as an advertising vehicle for his exercise apparatus. He had sold his interest in the oil burner concern, having decided to devote his full time to the mail-order business of selling instruction and apparatus.

Although Hoffman has had many imitators who have published magazines, books, and courses, and sold apparatus, he retained a lead in the field through his sponsorship of amateur weight lifting competition. He obtained employment in York for many promising lifters with the result that his York Barbell Club won U.S. team championships every year from 1932 to 1954, with the exception of 1952. In addition to bringing together the best lifters in the United States where they could train together and receive the stimulus of each other's competition, as well as share the benefit of their experience, he made generous financial contributions to AAU and Olympic funds. During non-Olympic years, he personally sponsored trips to Europe that resulted in four world championships for United States teams. Hoffman's support and development of U.S. weight lifting resulted in his being named coach of the 1948 and 1952 Olympic teams, both of which won the unofficial team scoring.

The first Olympics Hoffman witnessed were those held in Los

Angeles in 1932. On that occasion, American lifters had little respect from the more advanced Europeans. Only Tony Terlazzo and Henry Duey scored, winning third-place medals—Terlazzo in the 132-pound class and Duey in the 181-pound division. Terlazzo's total was 617 pounds and Duey scored with 727, lifting that is matched in many state championships today. Terlazzo continued to compete, however, and won the featherweight class in the 1936 games. Later he moved up to the lightweight class, but not before becoming the first American to set a world amateur weight lifting record. As a 148-pounder, Terlazzo made lifts that were unequalled for more than ten years, but which never received official international recognition because of Europe's unsettled state prior to World War II.

International rise of U.S. lifters

By the date scheduled for the 1940 Olympic Games, Bob Hoffman's York Barbell Club team alone was strong enough to have won nearly every class. In addition to Terlazzo, the club counted among its members Dick Bachtell, Bill Good, Wally Zagurski, Bob Mitchell, John Terpak, John Grimek, Steve Stanko, Dave Mayor, John Terry, John Davis, and others, all of whom had won, or placed, in U.S. championships. Terlazzo and Terpak had won world titles in 1937. Terlazzo won again and the sensational seventeen-year-old Davis won his first world championship as a lightheavyweight in 1938. Stanko placed second as a heavyweight the same year, but by 1940, he had progressed to the point where he could outlift any heavyweight in the world. During 1940, Davis and Terlazzo scored totals higher than the official records in their classes. Others of the U.S. champions, Terpak in the middleweight class and Terry, featherweight, seemed certain place-winners, if not gold medalists. It was unfortunate for American weight lifting that Europe's involvement in World War II kept this group from competing in the Olympic Games.

In 1941, Stanko passed a "psychological barrier." He made the first 1,000-pound three-lift total, and Davis soon moved into the heavyweight class and became the second man to score more than 1,000 pounds. Davis broke another barrier ten years later in 1951, when he cleaned and jerked 402 pounds officially. Although Rigoulot had lifted this much earlier, Davis was the first amateur to reach 400 pounds in competition using standard equipment.

Although the war lowered the level of U.S. weight lifting performances as it did throughout the world, the York club resumed activities, almost as if uninterrupted, after the cessation of hostilities. Davis had become an invincible heavyweight, and three years of army service in the Pacific seemed not to have affected his strength. The York club continued to dominate U.S. lifting with outstanding performances by world and national champions, like Stan Stanczyk, Frank Spellman, Joe Pitman, Emerick Ishikawa, Dave Sheppard, and Yas Kuzuhara, along with the veteran Davis.

But while the group from the medium-sized Pennsylvania Dutch manufacturing town was able to dominate U.S. team competition, great individual lifters, who often outscored York men in their classes and went on to world championships, developed throughout the country. Five outstanding men who developed into world champions and record-holders at widely separated points were: Joe DePietro, Pete George, Tommy Kono, Norbert Schemansky, and Paul Anderson. DePietro, a 58-inch "dwarf" with great strength and good coordination, represented the Bates Barbell Club of Paterson, N.J., and led the world's 123-pound class lifters to win the 1948 Olympic Games title. George, coached by the Barnholth brothers at the "American College of Modern Weight Lifting" in Akron, Ohio, became known as a "boy wonder," duplicating Davis' feat of winning a world title at seventeen. Kono, coached by Ed Yarick in Oakland, Calif., rose to win successive world titles at 148, 165, and 181 pounds, and set records in each division. Schemansky, a member of the Northern YMCA in Detroit, became the greatest of three strong brothers (the others, Dennis and Jerome, were U.S. champions) when he won world championships and set records as a middle heavyweight and a heavyweight. Schemansky was the first to defeat Davis in fifteen years when he beat him in 1953.

Anderson seemed, at first, a throw-back to the slow-moving lifter of the nineties, enjoying slow, grinding strength feats, such as the full squat—he performed ten repetitions with 700 pounds and six with 800! Although he weighed more than 300 pounds at 69½ inches in height, Anderson could move quickly when he wanted to and had good coordination. He refused football scholarships to several major universities in order to concentrate on weight lifting. In just three years of lifting, Anderson, at the age of 22, became the first lifter to score a 1,100 pound total on the three lifts. He pressed 375, snatched 320, and cleaned and jerked 405 in 1955. Later the same year, he officially pressed over 400 pounds and set a clean and jerk record of 436½. Anderson's measurements were a good indication that he could not be judged by ordinary standards. At the age of twenty-one, weighing 300 pounds, his wrists were huge at 9 inches, his ankles measured 11½ inches, and his knees measured 21 inches. He did carry considerable adipose tissue, but his arms, legs, and back were surprisingly solid for his size. Anderson's flexed upper arm measured 20¾ inches, neck 23 inches, normal chest 53 inches, waist 46½ inches, thighs 34 inches, and calves 19 inches! In addition to the standard lifts and heavy knee bending, he enjoyed practice of very heavy exercises, such as partial squats with 1,800 pounds on his shoulders and working one arm at a time by pressing a 200-pound dumbbell overhead.

Only one team was able to wrest group laurels from the York club from 1932 to 1954, and that was a well-trained Hawaiian aggregation managed by Dr. Richard You (1952 Olympic team physician). The Hawaiians were led by national champions Richard Tom (123) and Richard Tomita (132), and George Yoshioka and Ed Bailey, who were second at 123 and 198 pounds respectively. The only other team to rival the Pennsylvanians closely was that of Ed Yarick. The Californians won two classes, Mits Oshima at 132, and Kono at 165, and placed 198-pound Dan Uhalde second in 1953. In 1954, Oshima placed second to York's Kuzuhara, Jim Augustine (165) finished third, Art Jones placed second as a heavyweight, and Kono won at 181.

After World War II, Bob Hoffman continued his sponsorship of international teams. With Terpak retiring from competition to assist as manager-coach, after winning the world 181-pound title in 1947 and captaining the 1948 Olympic team, U.S. teams, sponsored by Hoffman, won world championships in 1946, 1947, 1950, and 1951. Hoffman also placed his financial support behind the victorious Olympic lifting teams of 1948 and 1952. Mainstays of the U.S. teams during these years were: DePietro, Tom, Bob Higgins, Kono, Stanczyk, Pitman, George, Sheppard, Spellman, Clyde Emrich, Davis, Schemansky, and Jim Bradford.

The greatest performance by the U.S. international team was on home soil, when the 1947 championships were held in Philadelphia. The home team won every class, with DePietro at 123, Higgins at 132, George at 148, Stanczyk at 165, Terpak at 181, and Davis far ahead as a heavyweight. At the 1948 Olympiad, DePietro won again, as did Stanczyk and Davis, and Frank Spellman won the middleweight class. George, Schemansky, and Harold Sakata placed second for the United States, and Richard Tom finished third as a bantamweight.

Russians rise as Egyptians fade

In 1946, the first team to represent Soviet Russia in a world championship appeared on the scene. Soundly beaten by the United States 11-9 (with Egypt scoring six points), although their amazing 63-inch lightheavyweight Novak set a world press record, the Russians returned home and did not appear again in international competition until 1949. On this occasion, they scored more points, 14, but were beaten by the U.S., with 18, and Egypt, with 15. They again dropped out of competition and did not return until 1952 when they believed their team was ready to defeat all comers. At the 1952 Olympiad, the Russian lifters showed they had definitely "arrived," although they did not quite match the Americans' performance. Davis won his second Olympic championship, Schemansky dominated the newly-sanctioned 198-pound class, and finished 77 pounds ahead of Novak, and George and Kono won the 165- and 148-pound classes. Bradford placed second to Davis, but Stanczyk suffered his first set-back in international lifting when he was beaten by Russia's Lomakin. It is interesting to note that all the gold medals were won by Americans (four) and Russians (three) and that no lifter but an American was able to beat a Russian. This marked the first year of a U.S.-Soviet international meeting in which no Egyptian was able to place as high as third.

With no nation but the United States able to produce a lifter who could beat a Russian, the following years were strictly a two-team battle for top honors. The state-supported Soviet team achieved its goal by winning the world team title in 1953, with the aid of a Canadian heavyweight named Doug Hepburn, who upset the injured Davis. Hepburn, one of the all-time strongest men, used his astounding shoulder and arm strength to take a lead in the press that Davis was unable to overtake in the quick lifts. An injured thigh held Davis 30 pounds below his limit in both the snatch and clean.

Although Schemansky, Kono, and George matched the three championships won by Udodov, Saxonov, and Vorobyev for Russia, the Soviet team scored more points in seconds and thirds. In 1954, the Russians widened their margin of victory with Vorobyev (198), Ivanov (148), Chimishkyan (132), and Farkhutdinov (123) winning individual championships. Again no one but an American was able to beat a Russian, Schemansky moving up to win as a heavyweight, Kono winning at 181, and George placing first at 165.

The 1955 meeting at Munich found almost the same team results, though with different men playing the starring roles in some classes. Russians Stogov (123), Chimishkyan (132), Kostylev (148), and Vorobyev (198) were first-place winners. Anderson (heavyweight), Kono (181), and Pete George (165) won for the United States. Earning seconds for the Soviet Union were Udodov (132), Bogdanovsky (165), and Stepanov (181). American entries to place were Bradford (second, heavyweight), Emrich (second, 198), Vinci (second, bantamweight), and Jim George (third, 181).

One noteworthy development of international lifting was the fact that heavier men from the western hemisphere have dominated their classes, while the lighter divisions have found Europeans and Asians consistently winning. A possible explanation for this may be the fact that the average American is taller than men from Middle Europe and Asia. A weight lifter, carrying all the useful muscle possible at an average height of about 69 inches, is almost certain to be no lighter in weight than 180 pounds, and men with larger bones usually develop into heavyweights at that height. With a tall national average, it seems that the chance of the United States developing world bantamweight and featherweight champions is much less than that of the shorter Europeans and Asians who have more small men from which to choose.

The internationalism of weight lifting, a sport in which the rules and equipment are the same in every part of the world, showed that no nation or race of people has a monopoly on athletic strongmen. With larger populations, countries like the United States and Russia of course have an advantage, but little Iran has produced a great champion in 123-pound Mahmoud Namdjou and a strong team to back him up. Egypt, with such champions as Ibrahim Shams, 148; Khadr El Touni, 165; Fayad, 132; and El Saied Nosseir, 181 and heavyweight, ranked among the leading weight lifting nations for 20 years. Rodney Wilkes and Lennox Kilgour were medalists in the Olympic games from the island of Trinidad, and Carlos Chavez, of Panama, closely approached the best lifting of the world's featherweights. In addition to its many great professionals, Germany has produced Haller, Liebsch, Ismayr, Wagner, and Manger, long holder of the world amateur heavyweight press record. Great Britain has been ably represented by Canada's Doug Hepburn and England's Ronald Walker, both of whom set world heavyweight records while at their best. From Argentina came two powerful heavyweights in Selvetti and Ferreira, with the former winning an Olympic bronze medal in 1952. Holland's Charite, Australia's Barberis, Sweden's Anderson, Burma's Maung, Korea's Kim, and the Philippine Islands' DelRosario have testified to the internationalism of weight lifting by ranking with the best in their classes. The foregoing is not an attempt to list the world's great amateur lifters, but is a list of outstanding men, selected at random, to show how widespread high level performance is in weight lifting.

The "Mr." contests

As a side attraction at the 1939 weight lifting championships, a "Mr. America" contest was held to determine the best developed man competing in the lifting meet. The event proved popular, was repeated annually, and was open to any registered AAU athlete. In 1940 and 1941, the winner was a former U.S. heavyweight champion and Olympic team member, John Grimek, whose amazing development was so outstanding that it was decided to prohibit former winners from re-entering. The contests were scored on a basis of points for muscle development, proportions, and general appearance, but for the most part it was large muscles with a small waistline that attracted the most attention. After the war, these contests became even more popular, with such international events, as "Mr. World" and "Mr. Universe," drawing large audiences. It was natural that these affairs should have an appeal, for most youngsters have dreamed of looking like "Mr. America" on the beach. They were sure this would bring them the admiration of the opposite sex and the envy of their fellow men.

Young men began practicing a specialized type of weight training intended to produce a startling body development— large chests, wide-spreading upper backs, small waistlines, and muscular arms and legs. Many youngsters wanted to emulate the "Mr." title winners and were exploited by equipment and course manufacturers, who taught "body beautiful" exercises (and sold apparatus) without attempting to make any transfer to truly competitive sports, such as weight lifting, track and field, wrestling, football, and the like. Best-developed-man contests were held in small towns and small sections of large metropolitan areas for such titles, as "Mr. Greenville" and "Mr. East Bronx." The young men, vying for these titles and the large trophies presented in the most inconsequential contests, exercised with the zeal of fanaticism.

In many cases, the winners of "Mr." contests, including the national events, were not athletic in movement and were sadly lacking in the strength that would be expected of men with such large muscles. They did not practice sports involving running or quick, coordinated movements, fearing that such vigorous activity might cause the shrinkage of a fraction of an inch in arm size. They did not exercise their muscles in coordinated weight lifting type movements, but concentrated on individual muscle groups, one at a time. They found they could "inflate" muscle tissue by many sets of moderately high repetitions with relatively light weights. This took time, so an appalling number of youngsters' only physical activity consisted solely of what grew to be termed "pumping up" their muscles. Gainful employment was taboo when it could be avoided because such activity interfered with developing the muscles. Lifting exercises to develop the strength of the loins and back also tend to increase the size of the hips and broaden the waistline somewhat, so extreme devotion to the ideals of "body building" probably cost the United

States many potential weight lifting champions. The wasp-waisted, broad-shouldered type usually lacks basic body strength because the lower back, hip, and side muscles are relatively under-developed.

Fortunately, the actual number of "muscle fanatics" was comparatively small when compared with persons practicing weight training as a physical conditioning hobby. The public posturing of the "body builders," however, had the unfortunate effect of convincing many casual observers that they were the sole end result of "weight lifting."

In defense of the "Mr." contests, it must be said that they served a worthwhile purpose in attracting many young men to weight training, an activity which enabled them to improve themselves physically. There have been some youngsters who have gone from body building to competitive weight lifting, others who have used "new-found" muscles to advantage in other sports, and still others who moderated their training to a healthful hobby.

Conditioning value of weight training

The public advocacy of weight training by such renowned athletes as Bob Richards, Parry O'Brien, Fortune Gordien, Dick Cleveland, Jack Kelly, Jr., Henry Wittenberg, and Frank Stranahan did much to offset bad publicity received by the "show-offs." The weight training activities of the above athletes will be discussed more fully in later chapters.

As many athletes began using resistance exercise to develop strength to help them excel at their favorite sports, competitive weight lifting gained in popularity. The most widespread use of barbells and dumbbells was as a "keep fit" activity practiced at home. Unfortunately there is no accurate record of the number of persons using weights at home to keep fit, but the York Barbell Company estimates most of its million-dollar gross annual business results from sales of barbell-dumbbell sets to private individuals. If only half this amount were spent for 100-pound barbell sets, it would mean that Americans were buying over thirty thousand home training sets a year!

Dr. Charles H. McCloy, professor of physical education at the State University of Iowa, believes it is the use of weight training at home that is its most valuable application. McCloy favors the teaching of weight training in schools and colleges because of its lifetime carry-over value. This form of exercise takes little time to effectively work the entire body vigorously, and requires little space. Barbell and/or dumbbell exercises can be practiced a few minutes daily in the privacy of a person's bedroom, and all the equipment needed can conveniently be stored by simply rolling it under a bed. McCloy contrasts this with other means of exercise, such as gymnastics, needing space and large apparatus; swimming, needing an expanse of water; and such sports as tennis, wrestling, and basketball, all of which require other participants as well as special facilities.

References

(*I*) BOOKS

(*1*) Calvert, Alan, *Super Strength*. Philadelphia: Milo Publishing Co., 1924.
(*2*) Hackenschmidt, George, *The Way to Live*. York, Pa.: Strength and Health Publishing Co.
(*3*) Hoffman, Bob, *Weight Lifting*. York, Pa.: Strength and Health Publishing Co., 1939.
(*4*) Mueller, Edgar, *Goerner the Mighty*. Leeds, England: Vulcan Publishing Co., 1951.
(*5*) Paschall, Harry B., *Bosco's Strength Notebook,* Vol. 1, No. 1. Alliance, Nebraska: Iron Man Publishing Company, 1951.
(*6*) ——, *Bosco's Strength Notebook,* Vol. 1, No. 2. Alliance, Nebraska: Iron Man Publishing Company.
(*7*) ——, *Development of Strength*. London: Vigour Press Ltd.
(*8*) ——, *Muscle Moulding*. London: Vigour Press Ltd.

(*II*) PERIODICALS (OR ARTICLES)

(*1*) Delaitte, Albert, "le Viennois Karl Swoboda," *Muscles,* p. 14, January, 1954, Andrimont, Belgium.
(*2*) Willoughby, David P., "Doug Hepburn—Is He a Second Louis Cyr?", *Your Physique,* p. 14, July, 1952, Your Physique Publishing Company, Montreal.

(*3*) Willoughby, David P., "How Strong Was Charles Rigoulot?", *Muscle Power*, p. 51, July, 1953, Muscle Power Publishing Company, Montreal.
(*4*) ——, "How Strong Was Arthur Saxon?", *Muscle Power*, p. 12, July, 1952, Muscle Power Publishing Company, Montreal.

(*III*) General Reference (issues from 1940 to 1955)

(*1*) *Strength and Health,* York, Pennsylvania.
(*2*) *Iron Man,* Alliance, Nebraska.

Part II

Chapter 2

The Men in the Sport

ONE of the most common criticisms leveled against dev- otees of weight training and body building is that they possess a narcissus complex. Like the mythical Greek youth, Narcissus, who fell in love with his own reflection observed in a pool of water, they are believed to be in love with their bodies. Instead of admiring their reflections in a pool of water, they supposedly spend hours in front of mirrors or strut in the semi-nude wherever they can show themselves before the public.

The criticism that weight lifters are afflicted with narcissus complexes can hardly be considered a serious one. Weight lifters who aim to break records would hardly have more time to spend in front of mirrors than any other non-lifter of their age. Those lifters, of course, who concentrate their efforts on body building and on winning Mr. Strongman contests, naturally have to practice in front of mirrors.

People in glass houses

A desire to show off is normal in the average young man. Many of them, while strutting on the beach, have regretted deeply that varsity letters were not emblazoned on their bare skins. Even if a young Hercules does proudly strut when he is in the field of vision of young damsels, or even of weak, flabby, obese, and otherwise discreditable samples of the male of our species, can you blame him very much? Before a stone is thrown at this Hercules, one should objectively weigh the pros and cons.

The acquired ugliness of the body is often the result of neglect on the part of its owner. This neglect is usually defended on the basis of the convenient philosophy that it is brains, and not brawn, that count. The acceptance of such a philosophy is made easier by the fact that a tailor can hide most body defects. One should remember that many a Hercules was not born with his strong body, but had to work hard and long to become what he now is. He did not like what he saw in the mirror and determined to look better. Now, since he has achieved that end, should we throw stones?

Are weight lifters dumbbells?

It is not uncommon to hear remarks that weight lifters are "muscle-bound between the ears," or have "strong bodies and weak minds." An "intellectual" who can barely lift the Unabridged Webster's Dictionary looks down upon a man who can easily carry the Encyclopaedia Britannica.

It is true that an "intellectual" teaching Latin or even journalism often looks down upon his colleague who teaches others how to utilize muscles. Some years ago, Professor Pitkin, in his book

The Twilight of the American Mind, referred to the intellectual level of instructors of physical education by saying, "Deep calls unto deep, dumbbells call unto dumbbells." If Pitkin said this about men using small dumbbells, one can imagine what he could have said about men using big barbells!

While it is possible that few, if any, champion lifters belong to learned societies or have high-sounding academic degrees, one should not forget that among the many thousands of men who zealously practice weight lifting and who represent a typical cross-section of the American population are to be found ministers, doctors, artists, and educators. You will also find all kinds of academic degrees attached to their names.

Since weight lifting has acquired noticeable popularity in colleges, it might be of interest to determine the mental level of students who participate in this activity. For this purpose, Zorbas and Karpovich (20)* obtained from three colleges the academic records of 392 students who were actively engaged in weight lifting. In all these colleges, the grading system was: A—Excellent, B—Good, C—Average. When the average grade for student lifters was calculated, it was found to be a little better than a B. Probably the same personal quality that enables a student to make himself study is also needed in order to make him stick to the systematic grind of weight training.

Who lifts weights in our country?

In periodicals dealing with weight lifting, pertinent information as to age and years of participation in this sport can be obtained only regarding very young, very old, or very outstanding performers. No census of *all* lifters has even been taken. For this reason, we have to depend on information, gathered by Karpovich (6), from 31,702 weight lifters.

---

* For the convenience of readers who may desire detailed discussions of the above and other studies, this and subsequent numbers refer to publications listed on pages 66 and 67.

This group may be considered as representative of the entire weight lifting population throughout the United States. Included in this group were men pursuing the weight lifting sport in YMCA's, in private clubs, in colleges and universities, and in one high school.

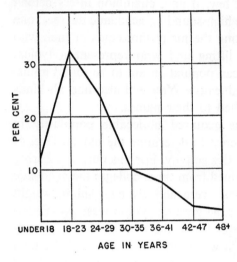

Figure 2. Ages of weight trainers and lifters.

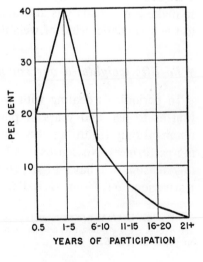

Figure 3. Number of years of participation in weight training and lifting.

From Figure 2 we may see that there was 12 per cent of participants under eighteen years of age. Between the ages of eighteen and twenty-three, the percentage increased to 32.5. This group was the largest. Then to be observed is a rather rapid decline until the age thirty–thirty-five is reached, after which the decline became more gradual. The group of forty-eight years and over, however, still represented 2.1 per cent. (There were two hundred and forty-six men over fifty-four years of age.)

From Figure 3 one may see the number of years of participation in weight lifting. Most individuals in the study, 39.5 per cent, had participated from one to five years. Then there was a sharp decline in numbers to 14.3 per cent for those who had participated from six to ten years. The decline continued so that the eleven-fifteen year group constituted 6.5 per cent of the total. The per cent for the sixteen-twenty year group was 2. There still were ten men who had participated more than twenty-one years.

Chapter 3

Muscles and Strength

OUR muscles are made up of small, thread-like muscle fibers. The fibers vary from $\frac{1}{25}$ to $1\frac{1}{2}$ inches in length and from $\frac{1}{250}$ to $\frac{1}{2500}$ inch in thickness. To form a big muscle, these fibers are arranged in bundles that extend in a chain-like fashion from one end of the muscle to the other. Each fiber and each bundle is wrapped in connective tissue, which is thin in flabby muscles and thick and tough in strong muscles. These wrappings are connected to each other, and at the ends of muscles they are fused with tendons, which in turn are attached to the bones. It has been estimated that there are about two hundred and fifty million muscle fibers in the body!

Under a microscope, one can see inside a fiber fine fibrils

that appear to have transverse stripes. Surrounding the fibrils is protoplasm, which in this case is called sarcoplasm. Near the surface of each fiber are several nuclei.

Each fiber is connected to one or two small nerve branches. For efficient functioning, a number of fibers receive branches from one and the same nerve. Because of this, they all contract or relax at the same time, working as a unit. For this reason, these groups of fibers are called *motor units*. In small muscles, such as in the muscles of the eyes, requiring fine adjustment, there may be as few as eight fibers in the unit. In muscles used for rather rough work such as muscles of the thigh, one may find one hundred or more fibers in a motor unit.

Each fiber is surrounded by a fine network of hair-like blood vessels called capillaries. This network is really amazing. If one takes a sliver of muscle as thin as the lead in an ordinary pencil and cuts across it, he will be able to count under a microscope from one hundred to four hundred capillaries in this small area. Such a great number of blood vessels around a fiber makes possible an abundant blood supply, a fast delivery of oxygen and nutriments, and an efficient removal of waste products.

When a muscle is resting, not all of the capillaries are open. They take turns in opening and closing. When a muscle is working to the limit of its capacity, all capillaries are open and the amount of blood brought to the muscle may be sixteen times greater than during rest.

Each muscle fiber contains a certain amount of stored energy in the form of *glycogen,* or animal starch. In a well-developed muscle, the amount of glycogen is about 1 per cent by weight.

According to measurements made on corpses, the weight of the biceps of both arms is about 1.4 pounds. In a living man, muscles of this size might contain over $\frac{2}{10}$ of an ounce of glycogen. This amount of glycogen could provide enough energy to curl 200 pounds thirteen times.

The weight of the biceps obtained from a corpse, of course, was much smaller than the weight of similar muscles in a well-developed weight lifter. For this reason, a weight lifter would have much more glycogen in his muscles. Moreover, curling is done not by the bicepses alone. Other muscles of the arms help in various degrees. It is safe to guess that a well-trained lifter has enough energy to curl 200 pounds twenty times or more. As far as it is known, nobody ever curled 200 pounds twenty times, because the waste products cannot be removed fast enough from the inside of the muscle fiber.

This illustration has been given for the following reason. Frequently, lifters take special "energy producing" stuff immediately before a contest. It may be honey, sugar pills, or other matter. The futility of such a practice is obvious. A lifter has more energy-giving glycogen in his muscles than he can possibly use in any contest. If one takes the extra energy supply, it will be just as effective if it were left in the locker instead of being put in the stomach.

From figures given in the foregoing discussion, one may easily calculate that if bicepses have enough potential energy to curl a 200-pound barbell thirteen times, there must be enough energy to curl 2,600 pounds once. Theoretically it is correct; however, there is a catch. Muscles cannot explode all the energy supply. There is a limit to the amount of energy that can be developed for a single contraction. Through training, muscles become bigger and are able to explode more energy at one time and, therefore, become stronger.

In a way, the situation is similar to the mechanism of a vending machine. If a machine delivers a piece of chocolate for a nickel, one has to place a nickel at a time and will get one chocolate bar each time. It will continue until the supply of chocolate has been exhausted. If you want to get more bars at each delivery, you have to rebuild the delivering mechanism. In the muscle, this rebuilding is achieved by training.

How muscles change during training

In training for strength, muscles increase in size much more than in training for endurance, because strength depends on the cross-section of muscle fibers, and endurance on the addition of capillaries around the fibers.

Although the size of muscles increases with exercise, the number of fibers remains the same. Obviously then, each fiber has to become larger. And that is what actually happens. Moreover, the connective membranes that envelop individual fibers and bundles of fibers become thicker and tougher, greatly adding to the bulk of the muscle. The tendons also become much stronger. One can easily see a relation between strength and structure by buying two cuts of meat, one cheap and the other expensive, taken from the same animal. The cheap cut, a section across the shin bone for example, will be tough, full of fibers, and will have to be boiled to be palatable; the expensive cut, say a tenderloin taken from a side, will be nice and tender and can be broiled as a steak. The cheap cut comes from muscles doing heavy work while the expensive cut comes from a more "privileged" type of muscle.

It is often disappointing for an athlete when he realizes that, although he trains as much as another fellow, his progress is slower. Whereas he is just fair, the other fellow may enter the champion class. It is hard to explain this difference. It probably depends on the original quality of muscle. One may occasionally meet a small, wiry man who exhibits enormous strength although his muscles are not bulky. On the other hand, some men with bulky muscles may not be as strong as one may have been led to believe.

How fast do muscles grow?

The answer depends on the individual differences and on the type and intensity of training. Although nothing can be done about individual differences with which man is endowed when he is born, the type and intensity of training can be controlled and adjusted to the individual.

Though there is no unanimous agreement regarding the details of training, there is one agreement in principle: if you want to develop strength, use the overload method. Use weights that are hard to lift. How hard? Agreement disappears here. Some would say, "Hard to lift more than five times," others, "Hard to lift more than ten times." If one wants to develop endurance, he should use light to medium weight and increase the number of repetitions. Scientific study of weight lifting started only recently, and on a small, timid scale. More investigation is needed. Meanwhile there is no other choice but to follow dogmatic rules set by an experienced trainer of your choice. This book utilizes the experience of many outstanding teachers.

In general, by exercising twice or three times per week for two months, one may expect an increase in the girth of his "biceps" from ⅝ to 1¼ inches; after four to six months, 1¾ to 2½ inches. After this period, the increase is much slower. The word "biceps" was put in quotation marks because actually the measure is of the largest circumference of the arm. Therefore, it measures also the increase in the size of the triceps, which lies on the side opposite to the biceps, and even of the brachialis muscle located in the inside of the arm.

The increase in the girth may also be due partially to an increase in the amount of fat under the skin. A lifter may add from 13 to 23 pounds of weight in two months and from 14 to 29 in five months. This increase is not all muscle.

Through the courtesy of Mr. Fraysher Ferguson of Apollo Studios, Columbus, Ohio, the authors present Table 1, showing changes in various body measurements that have occurred in some of his pupils during training.

TABLE 1

Changes of Body Measurements in Weight Training

Subject	1		2		3		4		5		6		7		8	
Duration of Training	2 Mo.		2 Mo.		2 Mo.		4 Mo.		5 Mo.		5 Mo.		5 Mo.		6 Mo.	
	Start	*Diff.*	*Start*	*Diff.*	*Start*	*Diff.*	*Start*	*Diff.*	*Start*	*Diff.*	*Start*	*Diff.*	*Start*	*Diff.*	*Start*	*Diff.*
Age	26		24		26		21		30		23		37		25	
Height	6'½"		6'3"		6'2"		5'10¼"		5'7¼"		6'¾"		6'1"		5'11¼"	
Weight	158	23½	186	13	185	18	122¼	21¼	138½	24½	152½	29	176	14½	137¾	34¼
Chest	42½	3	41½	2½	43	2¾	34½	2½	38	5	39¼	4¼	40	4½	33½	5¾
Waist	31	1	34½	½	34		28	2¼	30	2	30½	1½	33	1	28⅜	1⅝
Neck	15	¾	15½	½	16	1	13½	¾	15	¾	13¼	1¾	14½	¾	13⅝	1⅜
Biceps	13⅝	⅝	14	¾	14½	1¼	11¾	⅜	11⅞	1⅞	12¾	1¾	13¼	2½	11	2½
Forearm	11¾	½	12	¼	11¾	½	10⅞	⅜	10¾	⅞	11	1	11⅝	⅝	9¾	1¼
Wrist	7¼	—	7½	—	7⅜	⅛	7	—	6¾		6⅝	½	6⅞	⅜	6¼	½
Hips	38	1½	39	1	40	¾	34½	2½	37	3	38½	1¼	38½	1½	35½	2½
Thigh	22	1½	23½	¾	24½	1	19	2½	21	3	19	3	22½	2¼	20½	3

Courtesy of Mr. Fraysher Ferguson, Apollo Health Studios, Columbus, Ohio

How much does strength depend on weight?

It is well known that in general the heavier a man is the more weight he can lift. Therefore, for competitive purposes, contestants are divided into seven classes.

In the heavyweight class, where the sky is the limit, some lifters gorge themselves on ordinary or special food, believing that by gaining in body weight they will also gain in strength.

It is true some of the greatest weight lifters, both past and present, were very fat, weighing 300 pounds and more. The question arises: were they exceptionally strong because of this excess body weight or in spite of it? Since strength is a quality of muscles and not of fat, it must be concluded that excessively fat men may be strong in spite of fat.

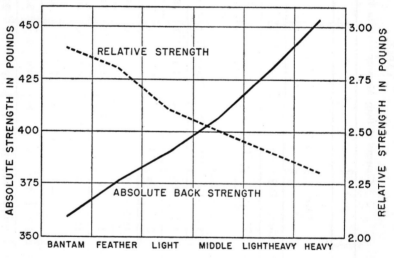

Figure 4. Relation between the relative and absolute strength of the back.

Suppose we measure the strength of the back muscles of men belonging to different body weight classes by asking them to pull with all their might on a dynamometer. The number of pounds of pull will indicate the *absolute strength* of the back muscles. If we divide the pounds of absolute strength by the body weight we will obtain the *relative strength* of the back muscles.

While the absolute strength increases with the increase in body weight, the relative strength decreases. This means that a man from a heavier class has relatively more nonmuscular tissue that a man from a lighter class. Figure 4, constructed on the basis of data given by Krestovnikoff (*11*), clearly illustrates the relation between absolute and relative strength.

Keeney (*9*) recently published an article showing the relation between the body weight, absolute strength, and relative strength for 114 contestants in the 1952 Olympic games, and for seven world champions.

As a measure of absolute strength, he took the total number of pounds lifted in the press, the snatch, and the clean and jerk. He expressed the relative strength in per cent of body weight:

$$\frac{S \times 100}{W}$$

S is the absolute strength and W is the body weight.

TABLE 2

Relation Between the Body Weight and the Total Load Lifted
(In Press, Snatch, and Clean and Jerk)

	1952 OLYMPIC MEN		1952 WORLD CHAMPIONS	
Body Weight	*Load Lifted*	$\frac{S}{W}$*	*Load Lifted*	$\frac{S}{W}$*
123	615.0	500	699	567
132	666.7	505	732.5	555
148	711.5	481	810	545
165	771.9	468	892.5	540
181	820.7	453	937	516
198	827.2	418	980.5	495

$*\frac{S}{W}$ = Load lifted in per cent of body weight.

Table 2 shows the relative strength of the Olympic contestants and the world champions. Dividing Keeney's S/W index by 100, we find how many pounds are lifted per one pound of body weight. In order to avoid confusion, we shall refer to this index as L/W, in which L is the load lifted and W is the body weight. It may be seen that the strength ratio for the champions is greater than for the Olympic contestants. This explains why they are champions.

It may be of interest to inspect the world championship totals for 1954, and compare them with the record made by Paul Anderson. (*See* Table 3.)   First, we observe that two men, Chimishkyan and Kono, have an S/W ratio unusually high for their respective classes. This makes them hard to beat. Comparing records of Anderson and Schemansky, we see that Anderson lifted 68 pounds more than Schemansky, but he also weighed 108 pounds more. Thus for each extra pound of weight, he lifted .63 pounds of extra load. One is tempted to predict that by the time Anderson becomes a 372 pounder he might lift 25 more pounds so that his record would become 1,167½. Although such a prediction may sound plausible, there are at least two flaws in it. First, with an additional gain in body weight the L/W for Anderson will become less than .63; therefore, he will need more than 40 pounds of body weight. Second, he might lose some weight and yet gain in strength.

TABLE 3

Relation Between the Body Weight and the Total Weight Lifted
(In Press, Snatch, and Clean and Jerk)

WORLD CHAMPIONS OF 1954 AND PAUL ANDERSON

Name and Country	Body Weight	Total Load Lifted	$\frac{S}{W}$ *
Farkhutdinov, U.S.S.R.	123	694	564.2
Chimishkyan, U.S.S.R.	132	771	584.0
Ivanov, U.S.S.R.	148	810	547.2
George, U.S.A.	165	892½	540.9
Kono, U.S.A.	172	958¾	557.4
Vorobyev, U.S.S.R.	198	1,014¼	512.3
Schemansky, U.S.A.	224	1,074¼	479.6
Paul Anderson, U. S. A.	332	1,142¼	344.0

* $\frac{S}{W}$ = Load lifted in per cent of body weight.

According to Keeney, the total load lifted in the three conventional lifts may be broken down as follows: Press: 30 per cent (29.5); Snatch: 31 per cent (30.85); Clean and Jerk: 40 per cent (39.63).

These proportions are applicable to all classes of body weight. The relation between the load lifted and the body weight of the lifter, however, cannot be expressed in a simple formula.* For this reason, the graph in Figure 5 has been prepared. This graph can serve as a guide to an aspirant for Olympic laurels.

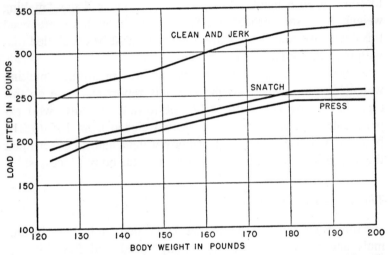

Figure 5. Relation between amount of load lifted by 1952 Olympic contestants and body weight.

If one bears in mind that human muscles, although working at great mechanical disadvantage because of shortness of bony power arms, can lift loads many times their own weight, it must be clear that when the lifting power increases less than the gain in body weight, this gain represents mostly inert, burdensome fat.

---

* Since the publication of this book, M. H. Lietzke has shown that there is a linear relationship between the logarithm of the weight lifted and the logarithm of the body weight. *Science*, 124: 486, 1956.

It seems that there is a point at which further gain in body weight will not lead to a gain in strength. Additional investigation into this weight-strength relationship is very desirable in order to determine at what point an increase in body weight becomes a handicap rather than an asset. This point must be at different levels for different people. Although there are champions who weigh over 300 pounds, there are also just fat men who weigh that much.

Infrequently, weight lifters take off a few pounds in order to compete in a lighter class. One may wonder if this "making weight" is a safe procedure. Since many men have practiced this device without any apparent harm, it must be concluded that within certain limits it must be safe.

There seem to be no scientific reports regarding "making weight" among weight lifters. The only report available on this topic is that by Dr. Tuttle (*18*) of Iowa University, who experimented on wrestlers. His subjects weighed from 145 to 217 pounds. A loss of 5 per cent of body weight had no effect upon the strength of the muscles and on the vital body processes.

The muscle-bound myth

From everyday experience, we know that body bulk in animals and men does not accompany speed and flexibility. A bulky draft horse will lose out to a race horse any day, and a circus contortionist, that miracle of flexibility, never has the body of a Hercules.

In discussing the effect of weight lifting upon speed and flexibility, attention is usually focused on men who belong to the heavyweight class. These men frequently have an excess of ballast, which may handicap them in all their body movements. However, the majority of weight lifters do not belong to this class. Actually many of them do not go after records but after body development, and refer to their sport as "weight training" rather than weight lifting.

Speed

Chui (2) reported that weight training for three months had a beneficial effect upon performance in tests requiring a combination of speed and strength. The tests consisted of the Sargent standing and running jump, and the shot put. Capen (1), on the other hand, after experimenting with college students, could only cautiously state that weight training "does not result in muscular tightness and in a decrease of speed of muscular contraction." The fact that Capen's weight lifters did not differ in their performance from the control group is to be explained obviously by the fact that the control group participated in a "very strenuous conditioning course" consisting of:

1. Tumbling.
2. Lifts and carries, hand-to-hand combat.
3. Conditioning gymnastics.

One may see that the weight lifting element in the activities given to the control group was quite considerable; therefore, the final results differed very little from those obtained by the weight lifting group.

Although short duration experiments may furnish valuable information, scientific and nonscientific curiosity is still aroused by the question: "What happens to weight lifters who have been engaged in this activity for several years?" For this reason, Zorbas and Karpovich undertook a study involving a large group of men. Six hundred persons, from eighteen to thirty years of age, were tested. Half of them had never indulged in weight lifting; the other half consisted of men who had participated in weight lifting for at least six months. Some of these latter men were tested at the 1950 National AAU Weight Lifting Championship Meet and at the Mr. America Contest held in Philadelphia in the same year. Some of the testing was done in private clubs in New York City and Western Massachusetts. Among those tested were champions from Australia, Hawaii, Puerto Rico, Canada, and from many states of this country.

Now a few words about the selection of the test. In weight lifting or weight training, arms receive relatively more attention than any other part of the body. The beginner watches his progress by observing changes in his "biceps." For this reason it was decided to test the speed of arm movement. Rotary movement was selected because it also involves large muscles of the chest and the back, and because it can be performed precisely. When the investigators tried just flexion and extension in the elbow joint, it was found that this movement could not be standardized because of a difference in the angle of flexion observed on a variety of individuals. A special instrument was devised for this test. This instrument automatically recorded the time of twenty-four complete rotary movements on an electrical stop watch. The movements were made in a clock-wise manner. Each man had two trials with a three-minute rest between trials. The better time was taken.

TABLE 4

Time Required for 24 Arm Revolutions by Weight Lifters
and Non-Weight Lifters

Group	Mean Time in Seconds	Excess Time over Group I
1. Weight Lifters	5.491	—
2. Non-Weight Lifters	5.665	.174
3. Springfield College	5.55	.06
4. Liberal Arts College	5.78	.29

From Research Quarterly, *22:148, 1951.*

Results of this testing were surprising to the investigators because they shared the opinion that intensive weight training slows down the speed of movements. From Table 4, one may see that the weight lifters were faster than the non-lifters. They needed 5.491 seconds for the test, whereas the non-lifters needed 5.665 seconds. Moreover, among the non-lifters, the students of Springfield College Physical Education Division were faster than the students from a liberal arts college. In both cases, the difference was statistically significant.

Later, Wilkins (*19*) demonstrated experimentally that training in weight lifting does not slow the speed, and Masley (*11*) showed that a greater increase in speed and coordination results from weight training than from volley ball.

Because of a beneficial effect of weight training, a track coach, I. L. Kintisch (*10*), has compiled a set of weight exercises he recommends for track and field athletes.

Flexibility

When Dr. Karpovich was a boy, he heard a story that a professional wrestler or strongman could not reach to scratch between his shoulder blades and had to pay a penny to some boy to do this scratching. When Karpovich became a physician, he was strongly opposed to weight lifting because he remembered this story, although he had never tried to verify it. Then an opportunity to test this story presented itself.

One day, Bob Hoffman visited Springfield College to give a lecture and to demonstrate weight lifting. He brought along John Grimek and John Davis. The lecture and demonstrations were very impressive. During the question period, the opportunity arose to test the legend. Very sweetly, Dr. Karpovich said, addressing Mr. Hoffman, "Will you please ask Mr. Grimek to scratch his back between the shoulder blades?" There was silence. Hoffman looked at Grimek, Grimek looked at Hoffman. Then they and everybody else looked at Dr. Karpovich.

Said Hoffman, "And why do you want Grimek to scratch his back?"

"Because I have been told that weight lifters are so musclebound that they cannot scratch their backs."

"Well, John," said Hoffman, addressing Grimek, "oblige the doctor and scratch your back." And Grimek did, first with one hand, then with the other. He scratched from above the shoulder and then from below. Davis did the same. The audience roared with laughter at the expense of Dr. Karpovich.

Both men had huge muscles and, therefore, *should have been* muscle-bound. But they were like the bumblebee who flies, although expert aviation engineers have proved mathematically that a bumblebee cannot fly. The anecdote only illustrates how strongly we may cling to our prejudices and pass on unfounded "information."

It is being recognized more and more that judicious weight lifting may aid in training for various sports. Elsewhere in this book will be found the names of outstanding athletes who have used weight training in developing muscles for their particular sport.

Of course, sometimes the reasoning for weight training assumes rather strange turns. We have met a coach who introduced barbell training for the arms of his track men. He had read an article by Dr. McCloy in which it was stated that there is a statistical relationship between the speed in running and the strength of the arms, the better runner having stronger arms. Although this may be true, the strength of the arms is a by-product of training and not the cause of greater speed in running.

You must have a plan to exercise properly

Everyone knows that if muscles are not given sufficient time for rest, they get tired and their strength temporarily goes down. Not everyone, however, knows that while one group of muscles is resting and the other muscle groups are exercising, the strength of the resting muscles may not only return to normal but actually become greater than at the beginning of the exercise.

For example, if one starts with a clean and jerk, then uses a press, and then chins himself on a bar, the strength of his hands may be weaker by 17 to 20 pounds by the end of the session. If, on the other hand, after using a clean and jerk, and a press, he performs squats, the strength of his hands may increase by 15 to 18 pounds. This increase is not caused by a mere rest period, but by an additional nerve stimulation—coming from working muscles.

How much time does it take?

It may be seen from Table 5 that the length of time actually spent on lifting is very short, the longest, 4.12 sec., being spent on a press and the shortest, 2.3 sec., on a snatch with one hand.

TABLE 5

Time in Seconds Spent on Different Phases in Weight Lifting

Kind of Lift	Weight Lifted in Pounds	Lift-ing on Chest	Hold-ing on Chest	Actual Moving Weight	Hold-ing on Straight Arms	Lower-ing Weight	Actual Lift-ing	Total
Press, Both Hands	143	1.36	1.69	2.76	1.4	2	4.12	9.21
Clean and Jerk, Both Hands	220	1.23	1.69	1+1.07*	1.53	2	3.30	8.62
Snatch, Both Hands	154			1.15+2.33	1.5	2	3.48	6.98
Clean and Jerk, One Hand	154	1.33	1.4	.97+1.30	1.5	2	3.60	8.5
Snatch, One Hand	121			1.23+1.07	1.5	2	2.30	5.8

From Krestovnikoff

* The first figure is the actual time of the lift and the second figure indicates the time spent on straightening of arms.

In every case, the lifting time is either about half of the total time or much less. Moreover, the rest pause at the chest is slightly longer than the time of lifting the weight to the chest. Even the rest pause at the end of a lift, when the weight is supported by the arms extended above the head, is longer than the time of actual lifting from the chest to that position. An exception is the press.

Although a training session may last from one to two hours, the actual time spent working with weights may not be more than two to six minutes. Most of the time is spent resting between the lifts. If we assume that the average total time spent, from the moment the weight is lifted from the floor until it is returned to the floor, is 7.5 seconds, the average resting time is about 4.5 minutes, or about thirty-six times longer than the actual time spent in lifting.

The importance of the proper length of rest periods between lifts cannot be emphasized too much. If it is too short or too long, it may ruin the chance for success. After a rest period of only thirty or forty seconds, most lifters fail to lift a heavier weight. A rest of from five to eleven minutes also lowers the ability to lift. The best resting time seems to be from three to five minutes.

Weight lifting without weights

One may meet many people who, while desiring to develop strong muscles, reject the idea of using weights. Instead of lifting dumbbells or barbells they use push-ups, chin-ups, sit-ups, etc., or use a set of springs, metal or rubber. Occasionally pulley weights are used because somehow they are different from other weights; but whether it is a barbell, or the weight of your own body or a spring, the physiological effect is the same.

Muscles work against resistance. This is all that counts. No system of physical education or a system of prophylactic or remedial exercises can exist without the use of resistance in one form or another (4, 5, and 12).

Chapter 4

Effects of Weight Lifting
on the Body

WATCHING a man weighing 132 lbs. clean and jerk a 245 lb. barbell, one is definitely impressed by his great exertion. Consequently, one may assume that the amount of energy used in weight lifting must be great. This assumption, if not clarified, may lead to wrong conclusions.

Energy used in weight lifting

Suppose that the height to which the 245 lbs. were lifted in a clean and jerk was six feet. The amount of work done in this case would be $245 \times 6 = 1470$ ft. lbs. The same amount of work would have been done if this man had merely climbed upstairs approximately 11 ft.—just one flight of stairs to the floor above.

Now, we can all make the second floor, even if we weigh much more than 132 lbs.; therefore, we can hardly be impressed by this "stunt." But here is the difference between walking upstairs and lifting by the clean and jerk: although a walk to a floor above may take fifteen seconds, the clean and jerk motions take only 3.30 seconds.

Thus, in this example, the intensity of work in lifting is 4.2 times greater than in walking. Calculating the amount of work in horse power, we obtain .76 for the lift and 0.18 horse power for climbing. The difference between these two activities, however, does not end here. In walking, the body weight is carried by the large muscle groups of the legs, while in lifting, the smaller muscle groups of the arms are also involved.

It has been observed that performance becomes less and less economical when the intensity of work increases. In the case of lifting, we observe that because of the smallness of the muscles of the arms, intensity greatly increases and efficiency decreases.* This fact makes lifting even more uneconomical.

Man carries weight upstairs more economically than he lifts barbells. This is because, in lifting barbells or weights, a smaller portion of the energy used is converted into work. Or, in other words, the mechanical efficiency of lifting weight is less than that of carrying weight upstairs.

In case the reader is not sure what is meant by efficiency, or speaking correctly, *mechanical efficiency,* it might be worth while to give a brief explanation. If energy used in an engine could be completely converted into useful work, the efficiency would be perfect, or 100 per cent. One hundred per cent efficiency never

---

* One should not get an impression that the authors forgot the fact that the lift involves action of many other muscles, including the legs. The brunt of lifting is still borne by the arms, especially in a press.

occurs. Even in the most economical motor, the efficiency is only about 30 per cent. In the human organism, efficiency occasionally may be as high as in a diesel engine, but ordinarily it is 25 per cent or less.

The lowest efficiency has been observed in swimming a crawl stroke. Even a good swimmer has efficiency as low as 2.5 per cent; for a poor swimmer, it is only 0.5 per cent.

The formulas for efficiency and energy are:

$$\textit{Formula I:} \text{ Efficiency (per cent)} = \frac{\text{Work} \times 100}{\text{Energy}}$$

Therefore:

$$\textit{Formula II:} \text{ Energy} = \frac{\text{Work} \times 100}{\text{Efficiency}}$$

Strange as it may seem, no data on the mechanical efficiency of weight lifting are to be found in available scientific literature. Material supplied by Krestovnikoff and based on research in Soviet Russia is incomplete and, therefore, cannot be safely used for calculation of efficiency. Because of this situation a research project has been started at Springfield College by a graduate student, Mr. Leslie Leggett. Although his study has not yet been completed, data obtained so far indicate that the mechanical efficiency of the three classic lifts is low, ranging from 3.6 to 6.06 per cent. In the calculations that follow, it will be assumed that the average efficiency of weight lifting is 5 per cent.

Let us apply Formula II to the previous discussion of walking a flight of stairs versus lifting. In both instances, the amount of work done was the same, namely 1,470 ft. lb. If we assume that the efficiency of climbing is 15 per cent, and the efficiency of lifting is 5 per cent, we obtain the following:

$$\frac{\text{Energy used in walking}}{\text{a flight of stairs}} = \frac{1{,}470 \text{ ft. lb.} \times 100}{15} = 9{,}800 \text{ ft. lbs.}$$

$$\frac{\text{Energy used in lifting}}{245 \text{ lbs.}} = \frac{1{,}470 \text{ ft. lb.} \times 100}{5} = 29{,}400 \text{ ft. lbs.}$$

Considerably more energy was used in lifting than in walking.

Let us now calculate how much energy could be used by a

132-lb. champion, Yas Kuzuhara, in one of his training sessions. Here is what he might do:

Press:	135 lbs.—Three Times	150 lbs.—Three Times
	175 lbs.—Three Times	190 lbs.—Two Times
	200 lbs.—Two Times	210 lbs.—One Time
	200 lbs.—One Time	190 lbs.—Six Times
Snatch:	135 lbs.—Three Times	150 lbs.—Three Times
	170 lbs.—Three Times	180 lbs.—Two Times
	190 lbs.—One Time	200 lbs.—One Time
Clean and Jerk:	185 lbs.—Three Times	205 lbs.—Three Times
	225 lbs.—Two Times	245 lbs.—Two Times
Pull to Waist Height:	225 lbs.—Three Times	245 lbs.—Three Times
	255 lbs.—Nine Times	

The total amount of work done was 44,078 ft. lbs. The same amount of work would have been done if Mr. Kuzuhara had climbed to the 34th floor of a skyscraper. Assuming that the mechanical efficiency of his weight lifting was 5 per cent, the amount of energy spent on lifting was equivalent to:

$$\frac{44,078 \times 100}{5} = 881,560 \text{ ft. lbs.}$$

If this energy had been used for stair climbing, Mr. Kuzuhara could have walked to the 101th floor of a skyscraper.

Let us now express the amount of energy used by him in calories. Since one calorie is equivalent to 3,086 ft. lbs., 881,560 ft. lbs. will be equivalent to 286 calories. This figure looks less impressive than the figure indicating the foot-pounds of work. As a matter of fact, slightly more than this number of calories is obtained from a light breakfast consisting of one slice of toast and a glass of milk.

During one well-conducted experimental training session, the average amount of energy used was 234 calories. One can easily see that, since most weight lifters have an appetite which may cause them to eat in excess of their need, the extra food may make them fat in spite of exercise. This is especially true when a lifter discontinues his training because his appetite remains the same but the amount of energy needed becomes less.

Weight lifting and pulse rate

At the beginning of this century, Dr. James H. McCurdy (*15*) performed a series of experiments to determine how the heart reacts to a maximum sustained effort. The subject sat on a chair with his right hand under the seat of the chair. On a given signal, the subject would hold his breath and then pull with all his might with the right arm. During this pull, the pulse and blood pressure were taken. Tests were also given to subjects exerting a maximum pull on a leg and back dynamometer.

McCurdy found that while, on the average, the blood pressure increased by 69 mm. of mercury (on one occasion it increased by 160 mm.), the heart rate was practically unchanged. Eventually McCurdy's experiments were interpreted as proving that during *weight lifting* the pulse rate does not change, while blood pressure is greatly increased. This incorrect interpretation continued for fifty years. In McCurdy's experiment, there was no actual lift. The subjects attempted to lift themselves, so to speak, by "their own bootstraps." The effort exerted in such an action represents only one part of lifting. When a weight is actually lifted, the muscles go through a dynamic contraction instead of executing merely a sustained static contraction.

Numerous observations made by Russian investigators during training and contests have shown that the pulse rate is affected very much. For a press, the increase is 76.1 per cent, for a clean and jerk, 88.8 per cent, and for a snatch, 98.7 per cent.

During a contest, the resting pulse rate is faster than normal because of the emotional factors involved. The effect of the excitement may be ascertained by comparing the resting pulse before or during the contest with that on a day preceding the contest. During the contest, the pulse rate may be increased as much as 68 per cent. For this reason, resting pulse rate data obtained on weight lifters during a contest do not represent the normal figures and should be supplemented by data gathered several days before or after a contest. Figure 6 clearly illustrates this point.

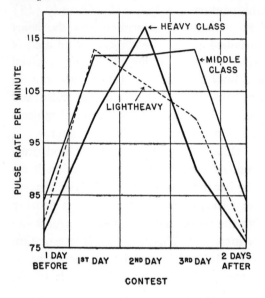

Figure 6. Emotional effect of weight lifting contest upon pulse rate.

Weight lifting and blood pressure

Arterial blood pressure is also greatly affected during weight lifting. The following conclusions may be drawn from measurements made immediately after lifting: the systolic pressure is always increased, and the diastolic may remain the same, may go down, or may slightly rise. The behavior of the diastolic pressure probably depends on the type of lift.

Table 6, made from the data obtained by Dr. Ziegler, shows that after ten repetitions of a split snatch, the diastolic pressure always went down. In a boy sixteen years of age, it dropped from 82 mm. of mercury to 20 mm.

The excitement of a contest also affects the blood pressure. The average pressure obtained on all classes of weight lifters showed that the day before the contest, arterial blood pressure was 116/58; on the first day of the contest, 129/54; on the second day, 140/66; on the third day, 146/64; and only two days after the contest did it come back to normal, 120/55.

TABLE 6

Effect of Ten Repetitions of Split Snatches upon
the Pulse Rate and Blood Pressure

| SUBJECT | Weight lb. | Age | Ht. | Wt. | BEFORE | | IMMEDIATELY | | 5 MIN. AFTER | | 10 MIN. AFTER | |
					P	BP	P	BP	P	BP	P	BP
J. T. Sr.	115	42	66.5	169	78	120/80	152	170/60	100	130/90	70	120/70
J. T. Jr.	100	16	68	150	100	118/82	150	140/20	120	130/50	90	90/70
R. B.	100	47	63	140		115/80		150/30				100/70
J. B.	115	37	68	180		120/80		140/50		120/80		110/80
J. P.	135	27	69.5	190		130/70	125	160/40	85	130/70	70	120/70
J. M.	135	28	72.5	207	80	120/80	85	150/60	80	125/75		

Courtesy of Dr. John B. Ziegler, Olney, Md.

The amount of increase and the time needed for return to normal of the pulse rate and systolic blood pressure after a snatch has been proposed by Ermolaiev as a test of physical condition of weight lifters. The lower the rise and the shorter the time needed for recovery, the better is the condition.

The rise in systolic blood pressure during a lift needs additional explanation. When a person is lifting a weight, he stops breathing. In this manner, the chest becomes stabilized and more force can be developed by the muscles. The muscles of the chest and abdomen are contracted during a lift, and they exert great pressure upon the chest and the abdomen. The immediate effect of this increased pressure is that the systolic blood pressure rises abruptly. Since the increased pressure in the chest and abdomen interferes with the return of the venous blood to the heart, the arterial blood pressure may suddenly drop to 90 mm. and the person may faint, or it may remain high and the person will not faint. This change in the blood pressure during straining has been proposed as a test of the condition of athletes. Although, generally speaking, the test may detect large differences between individuals, it has been observed that even strong men in good condition occasionally fainted during this test.

Prolonged breath holding while straining during a press or even while trying to show off during a "Mr. Strongman" exhibition has been responsible for fainting of contestants.

The possibility of a great rise in systolic blood pressure during weight lifting has always been considered as a strike against weight lifting. It has been assumed that this strain may damage the heart. Although one cannot deny that the strain of weight lifting cannot be recommended for people with heart and blood vessel disease, there has never been convincing evidence presented that straining was injurious to a normal heart.

Although there are many occasions in daily life that require straining, such as reaching, digging, or shoveling, they are done without injury to the normal heart. A person in a coughing, laughing, or sneezing fit may even exert considerable strain without any apparent ill effect upon the heart.

What should the athlete eat?

Any weight lifter knows that the strength and power he seeks comes from the food he eats. He may be paying a great deal of attention to what he eats and may actually be worrying about his diet. With television, radio, and printed matter persistently advertising energy-giving and body-building foods, he cannot help being aware of differences, real or imaginary, in the properties of food ingredients.

When he finds out that proteins are needed for building and maintenance of body tissues, he realizes that, since his muscles must grow, he needs a great deal of protein for these muscles. Then, when he discovers that the energy-giving foods differ in the amounts of energy they contain per unit of weights, by analogy he begins to think about the energy-giving foods in the same terms as he thinks about gasoline. With a poor, low-octane gasoline, his car will be sluggish and the motor will cough and sputter. With a good, high-octane gas, the motor will hum happily while he breaks all speed limits.

If this analogy is applied to the foods Man eats, we may say that low-octane substances are vegetables and fruits. High-octane foods are those that contain less water; for example, peas or beans, meat, and sugar. The highest-octane value will be found in butter, oils, and fats.

Here the analogy between gas and food ends, for Man cannot select food on such a simple basis. The low-octane vegetables and fruits are needed for their vitamin and mineral content. Presence of large amounts of water does not make vegetables less desirable because Man needs water too. The more vegetables taken in, the less one will need to drink water.

One may ask: is there not some food stuff especially beneficial to an athlete? From time to time, various foods are promoted as miraculous sources of energy. About thirty years ago it was sugar. It had been observed that some of the Boston Marathon runners who did poorly had subnormal amounts of sugar in the blood. When, during subsequent races, the men were given sugar, their performance improved. As a result of this observation, sugar and other sweet substances, including candy, came into great prominence in the athletic world.

A story was circulated about a famous football coach who gave one of his players a quarter of a pound of sugar before a game. The man became ill with an acute upset stomach. One should be cautious not to eat too many sweets. Although sugar and sweets may be considered as good emergency food, there is enough sugar in everyday food for usual athletic performances.

Fifteen years ago it was gelatine that suddenly acquired national and international notoriety. This familiar substance, used for making Jello and jelly salads, overnight became a miracle food that could make a man more energetic, delay fatigue, and hasten recovery from fatigue. Athletes throughout the United States started using gelatine, and coaches testified to the wonderful effects this substance had on their players.

This sudden fame of gelatine had resulted from an honest mistake made in a reputable laboratory. When this mistake was finally discovered (7), gelatine left the medicine cabinet and locker room and went back where it belonged, in the kitchen.

A few years ago, the high protein diet came to the fore. This was not a new bid for fame as far as protein was concerned. There had been a time when protein was considered the best source of energy for muscles. Later it had been relegated to second place, being advocated mainly as a body-builder, not an energy-giver. About twenty years ago, a British physiologist published an account of his research, indicating the beneficial effect of high protein diet in training. His findings, however, have not been verified by other investigation. After World War II, when this country tried to feed the rest of the world, the importance of expensive proteins again came to the foreground. Meanwhile scientific articles had started to appear indicating that proteins do take part in producing energy during muscular work. Although the quantity needed is small, the part played has been shown to be important.

In 1951, an article (16) appeared in a Russian physiological journal stating that rats undergoing training in swimming receiving a small addition of protein to their usual normal diet, developed bigger and stronger muscles. Since no analysis of the ordinary diet has been given in the article, we do not know whether their ordinary diet was adequate or not. For this reason, the whole experiment cannot be considered as objective.

Meanwhile rumors have been reaching us that Russian weight lifters who have done so well in international contests have been using a high protein diet. Whether it is true or not, the authors of this book do not know. Perhaps they only get more protein than other Russians. But it really does not matter as will be shown very shortly.

At the present time, another food substance is beginning to get notoriety—wheat germ oil. During the past few years, this oil has been used by various athletes because of its supposedly miraculous effects. Experiments on swimmers (3) failed to support the faith in the wheat germ oil.

It seems, therefore, that wheat germ oil will join the company of another vitamin, vitamin B_1, which has had its short lived fame as a miracle aid to athletes, particularly swimmers. Those interested in the athletic story of vitamin B_1 will find references (8 and 14) at the end of this part.

So far, this chapter has only been debunking notions and misconceptions. What about constructive guides to a good diet for a weight lifter? The reader must prepare himself for a disappointment. To lessen this disappointment, let us consider a few obvious facts.

We know that no single country has a monopoly on champions. Not only large countries but countries as small as Estonia and Latvia, each with populations of less than two million people, have had weight lifting champions. Now let us make an imaginary trip and visit, say, Olympic teams during their meal time. The only common sight on the tables will be a generous quantity of food. Otherwise, the outward similarity seems to end.

Weight lifters coming from different countries will follow their native tastes and will eat foods typical of their countries. What one man will eat with zest in one country, may look and taste repulsive to a man from another country. A Dutchman may eat a fresh herring with gusto, but an East Indian (even a meat eater) may refuse to touch one because herring is "raw fish."

Although a Finn or Estonian will eat with pleasure a bowl of sour milk with a thick layer of sour cream, another man would refuse it because sour milk to him is spoiled milk.

And then as to meat: some like beef, some like lamb, and some avoid both beef and lamb. Some people will eat pork and some will feel nauseated at the sight of pork. And so on.

Yet, in spite of all this variety, there are several characteristics common to all diets. The bulk of the diet of any weight lifter, no matter where he comes from, consists of carbohydrates, whether it be bread, potatoes, rice, spaghetti, or vegetables. All weight lifters get approximately the same amount of proteins, which come from all kinds of meat, poultry, fish, beans, peas, cheese, or milk. The amount of fat, however, varies a great deal. Some people like fat, and use it in large quantities and take it in various forms, up to one third of a pound. The fat comes in butter, milk, bacon, ham, lamb chops, salad oil, and foods of that nature.

One third of a pound of fat per day may sound too much, but it is not, according to leading dietitians, who recommend from 25 to 35 per cent of an athlete's intake of calories in the form of fat. A weight lifter may need 4,000 calories per day. Twenty-five and 35 per cent will make 1,000 and 1,400 calories respectively. These amounts of calories may be obtained from about 4 to 5.4 oz. of lard or 5 to 6.6 oz. of butter or margarine.

Some lifters try to avoid fat and fatty foods. In spite of their efforts, they probably take in about a quarter of a pound of fat a day.

All these men, regardless of apparent differences in diets, may become champions. So what should a weight lifter eat?

This question must be restated: What should most American weight lifters eat? Even in this form, the question is rather difficult to answer, because American athletes are influenced by their national origin and by the states in which they were brought up.

It must be stated now that there is *no special diet* for weight lifters. Their diet is the same as for any man engaged in relatively hard muscular work. A lifter who earns his living by doing physical work will need between 3,500 and 4,500 calories per day, depending on the size of his body and the intensity of training.

In order to insure an adequate diet, one may follow suggestions made by The Food and Nutrition Board of the National Research Council:

Milk—Two or more glasses.
Vegetables—Two or more servings besides potato; raw green and yellow vegetables should be used.
Fruits and tomatoes—Two or more daily.
Eggs—One a day.
Meat, cheese, fish, or peas and beans.
Cereal or bread—Preferably whole grain or enriched.
Butter or margarine—Two or three pats daily.

The amount of meat or poultry one should eat will be governed by one's pocketbook and taste. If other protein foods are used, one will not need more than one half a pound of meat. The same is true about fish. As to the bread, one again may be guided by his appetite.

During an experiment conducted by Dr. Karpovich (7) in a county jail, a group of inmates had to ride stationary bicycles with brakes on. They did it five times a week and developed tremendous endurance. One man, for instance, could ride continuously over six hours, when at the beginning, his limit was ten minutes. He needed a source of energy for his work, and bread was the only food he could use in unlimited quantity. For breakfast he ate 12 to 14 slices; for lunch 14 to 19; and for dinner 23 to 25 slices. This man, by the way, neither gained nor lost weight.

In what form foods listed above are taken does not matter unless one is sick or has a "delicate" stomach. Although broiled meat and fish take less time for digestion, the length of digestion time is of no particular importance except on the day of a contest. If one lifter likes pigs knuckles and sauerkraut and another prefers baked beans, nothing can be said against these meals except that it is better to avoid them on the day of a contest. (These two meals may be responsible for excessive intestinal gas, making straining uncomfortable.)

The question is frequently raised: Should a lifter eat fried potatoes or doughnuts? Perhaps he should not, but he can eat them without any ill effects. From a standpoint of good nutrition, however, a baked potato is preferable to French fries, and a slice of bread with jam may be better than a doughnut. Nonetheless, some people do not like jam, and not many of us would enjoy eating baked potatoes all the time.

If one follows the suggestions made above, there will be no need for vitamin pills. There will be no particular need for canned high-protein food either. One can get his proteins in a less expensive form by buying cheaper cuts of meat or by using peas and beans.

With a healthy appetite, a lifter should watch his weight. If he gains too rapidly, he may be putting on fat instead of muscles.

Injuries in weight lifting

One of the main reasons why physical educators and physicians object to weight lifting is the belief that this activity is dangerous to the life and limb of the participant. According to this belief, a weight lifter is in constant danger of wrenching his back, or pulling or even rupturing muscles and tendons. Besides this, the strain is considered likely to cause a hernia or damage to the heart.

It is true that accidents do happen in weight lifting. Muscles may be ruptured; hands and feet and even the head may be crushed. But how often do these accidents occur? Until 1949, nobody seemed to be interested in obtaining statistics on injuries caused by weight lifting. That year Dr. Rudd (17) made a study in which he questioned weight lifters, orthopedic surgeons, and cardiologists in the Boston area. He found that accidents were rare and that no heart specialist could recall any weight lifter who had been his patient.

In 1950, Dr. Karpovich (6), in cooperation with the National YMCA Physical Education Council and the *Iron Man* and *Strength and Health* magazines, sent questionnaires to all YMCA's and some private clubs and colleges. Replies were received from 111 YMCA's, five private clubs, five colleges, and one high school. They covered the incidence of injuries that occurred during 1949–50, among 31,702 participants.

The total number of injuries reported was 494 or 1.5 per cent of the participants. Most injuries consisted of "pulled" muscles and tendons. Table 7 shows the breakdown according to the part of the body injured and the incidence of a few types of injuries. One may observe that the back and wrists were the parts of the body most frequently affected. Attention is called to the complete absence of reports concerning heart injuries on the part of those physicians.

TABLE 7

Incidence of Injuries Among 31,702 Men Participating
in Weight Lifting *

Fingers	74	Feet	15
Wrists	96	Ruptured muscles	19
Arms	8	Heart	0
Shoulders	77	Varicose veins in arms	16
Back	100	Hemorrhoids	19
Thigh	17	Hernias	5
Knees	31	Collapse	1
Ankles	15	Sudden death	1

TOTAL NUMBER OF INJURIES .... 494 or 1.5%

* Most of the injuries consisted of "pulled" muscles and tendons.

Journal of Physical Education, *48:21, 1951.*

Although, from a theoretical standpoint, a strain during weight lifting *should* favor development of a hernia, the reported figures indicate that hernias among weight lifters are rare. According to a report based on the Selective Service Examination during World War II, the incidence of hernias among young people in the United States is 64.4 cases per one thousand men. Thus we could expect 103 cases of hernias among 31,702 men. Instead there were only five cases, twenty times fewer than among an average selection of people.

Anyone who has used questionnaires for collecting information knows that one cannot rely too much on this type of material. For this reason, a personal check-up of seventy-five weight lifters was made. This check-up revealed that, in 1949–50, the incidence of injuries was 4.5 per cent. This figure, although larger than that obtained from questionnaires, is still too small for condemning weight lifting as a dangerous sport. Moreover, most injuries were of a trivial nature.

While speaking about injuries occurring in weight lifting, one should not forget that some of them are caused by accidents that could have been prevented. Although a pulled tendon or fractured toe might be considered a "legitimate" accident, it would require some planning to break a head or a neck. Usually such accidents are the result of the ingenuity of a local genius who has built a flimsy weight rack or some sort of Rube Goldberg contraption for lifting weights while lying underneath in a frame. The management and members of weight training clubs should be on constant guard against all flimsy and suspicious-looking devices. Although fatal accidents are rare, one accident is all that is needed for one man.

Warning also should be sounded against taping hands to the shaft of the barbell. Taping makes possible the lifting of a heavier weight, but it has been responsible also for serious accidents, as when a man could not retain the weight at straight arms, lost his balance and fell backwards. The accident record in weight lifting clubs, fortunately, has been very low and it should remain so.

References

(1) PERIODICALS

(1) Capen, E. K., "The Effect of Systematic Weight Training on Power, Strength, and Endurance," *Research Quarterly*, 21:83, 1950.
(2) Chui, E., "The Effect of Systematic Weight Training on Athletic Power," *Research Quarterly*, 21:188, 1950.

(3) Cureton, T. K., "Wheat Germ Oil, the 'Wonder' Fuel," *Scholastic Coach*, p. 36, March, 1955.

(4) DeLorme, Thomas L., "Restoration of Muscle Power by Heavy-Resistance Exercises," *Journal of Bone and Joint Surgery*, 27:645, 1945.

(5) Gallagher, J. R. and T. L. DeLorme, "The Use of the Technique of Progressive Resistance Exercise in Adolescence," *Journal of Bone and Joint Surgery*, 31:847, 1949.

(6) Karpovich, P. V., "Incidence of Injuries in Weight Lifting," *Journal of Physical Education*, 48:81, 1951.

(7) ——— and K. Pestrecov, "Effect of Gelatin upon Muscular Work in Man," *American Journal of Physiology*, 134:300, 1941.

(8) ——— and N. Millman, "Vitamin B_1 and Endurance," *New England Journal of Medicine*, 226:881, 1942.

(9) Keeney, C. E., "Relationship of Body Weight to Strength–Body Weight Ratio in Championship Weight Lifters," *Research Quarterly*, 26:54, 1955.

(10) Kintisch, I. L., "Weight Training for Weight Men," *Scholastic Coach*, p. 7, Feb., 1955.

(11) Krestovnikoff, A. P., "Fiziologia Sporta," *Fizkultura and Sport*, Moscow, 1939.

(12) Kusinitz, I., "A United States Air Force Physical Reconditioning Program," *Journal of the Association for Physical and Mental Rehabilitation*, 8:75, 1954.

(13) Masley, J. W., "Weight Training in Relation to Strength, Speed, and Coordination," *Research Quarterly*, 24:308-315, 1953.

(14) McCormick, W. J., "Vitamin B_1 and Physical Endurance," *Medical Record*, 152:439, 1940.

(15) McCurdy, J. H., "The Effect of Maximum Muscular Effort on Blood Pressure," *American Journal of Physiology*, 5:95, 1901.

(16) Popova, N. K., "Effect of Muscular Activity upon the Utilization of Nitrogenous Substances," *Fiziologitchesky Zhurnal*, 37:103, 1951.

(17) Rudd, J., "Weight Lifting—Healthful—Harmful?" *Journal of Physical Education*, 46:90, 1949.

(18) Tuttle, W. W., "The Effect of Weight Loss by Dehydration and the Withholding of Food on the Physiologic Responses of Wrestlers," *Research Quarterly*, 14:159, 1943.

(19) Wilkins, B. M., "The Effect of Weight Training on Speed of Movement," *Research Quarterly*, 23:361-369, 1952.

(20) Zorbas, William S. and P. V. Karpovich, "The Effect of Weight Lifting Upon the Speed of Muscular Contractions," *Research Quarterly*, 22:148, 1951.

(3) CURETON, T. K., "Have Dares Out the Wonder Foot," pamphlet, C. H. Stoelting Co.

(4) CALHOON, HENRY L., "Mechanism of Muscle Power by Heat," Amer. Jour. Physiol., reprint of Ross and John, Interjoy, 71 163.

(5) CALHOON, Edmund E. H., Lima, "The Use of the Technique of Conditioned Reflex in Arteriosclerotic Disease of Heart and Aorta," Amer. J. Sci., 1949.

(6) KRAMRAUCH, L. V., "Incidence of Infants in Vegan Babies," Jour. of Pediatrics, 36 181, 1951.

(7) ——— and K. KRUKMAN, "Effect of Obesity upon Muscular Work," Inter. J. Physiol., Journal of Physiology, 157 256, 1951.

(8) ——— E. M., "Minimum Vitamin B₁ and B₂ Intake in Humans," Journal of Nutrition, 32 181, 1947.

(9) KRAUSE, T. K., "Maintenance of Body Weight in Strength Training," Bulletin of American Weight Lifting Association, September, 1944.

(10) CURETON, T. K., "Weight Training for Weight Men," Athletic Journal, Feb. 1944.

(11) RASMUSSEN, A. P., "Metabolic Sports," Athenæum and Sport Medicine, 1940.

(12) KRAINES, E., "A United States Air Force, Physical Reconditioning Program," Journal of the Association for Physical and Mental Health, November, 1942.

(13) MACKAY, "Weight Training in Relation to Human Speed and Coordination," Journal of Quant. Biol., 34 392 115, 1944.

(14) MCCLOY, C. H., "Health, Fitness, and Physical Endurance," Science, 12 113, 1943.

(15) MURPHY, J. H., "The Facts of Maximum Strength," Jour. Lab. Clin. Science, American Journal of Physiology, 295, 1934.

(16) PEALE, N. K., "Effect of Moderate Activity upon the Condition of Pulmonary Substances," Physiological Review, 17 103, 1931.

(17) ——— "Weight Lifting—Strength—Exercise," Federation Proceedings, June, 1948.

(18) TUTTLE, W. W., "The Effect of Weight Loss by Isolation on the Whole Relation of Food on the Physiologic Response in Humans," J. Amer. Geriat., 11 175, 1945.

(19) WILKIE, H. H., "The Effect of Weight Training on Speed of Movement," Research Quarterly, 23 361 362, 1942.

(20) WILKIE, ALFRED WILLIAMS, and FAY REYNOLDS, "The Effect of Weight Training Upon the Speed of Muscular Contraction," Research Quarterly, 23 148, 1951.

Part III

Chapter 5

Basic Conditioning and Strengthening Through Resistance Exercise

THE average physical education teacher or athletic coach will have little, if any, interest in turning out the rippling-muscled specimens who compete in annual "Mr. America" contests and similar best-developed-man events. He will, however, often have students who need special attention to gain the strength to which every man is entitled, or team prospects who would perform more efficiently by the simple addition of strength. The basic exercises to be described in this chapter are

71

not new or different from movements weight-trained men have
been practicing for decades, but they do solve the problem of
adding strength and increasing the size of all the body's muscles,
and therefore have their part in a physical conditioning program. (*See* Figures 7 *and* 8.)

The system of progression is simple. It is one in which the
muscles are trained to do more and more work gradually. The
increase of strength is the first improvement a newcomer to
weight training will notice. Development of muscle or improvement of body proportions is incidental and slower of accom-
plishment. Gains in both strength and muscle size, however,
will be relatively rapid at the start and slower after progress
has been made.

To develop strength and improve muscle tone of the smaller
muscle groups of the arms, shoulders, upper back, and chest, it
has been found that progression from eight to twelve repetitions
with a given weight, before increasing resistance, brings good
results. That is, a person beginning barbell training (or dumbbell training, or both) should experiment to determine how
much weight he can use to perform a given exercise eight repetitions without stopping. Exercising only every other day, or
three alternating days per week (example: Monday, Wednesday, and Friday), he should attempt to add a repetition with
each training period. When he reaches twelve repetitions, he
should add 5 or 10 pounds to the barbell and drop back to
eight repetitions to begin the same upward progression of first
repetitions and then weight.

This, obviously, is a program of gradually increasing severity.
It is so gradual as to make injury or overwork almost impossible.

The larger muscles of the legs and lower back usually require
more repetitions and can stand greater weight increases than
the arms and upper body. In working the lower body and legs, it
has been found advisable, through practical experience, to work
up from ten to fifteen or eighteen repetitions and then add 10
or 20 pounds.

Obviously there is a limit to how far a human being can go with this kind of progress. Otherwise we could all be pressing 500 pounds overhead in a matter of months. When a "sticking

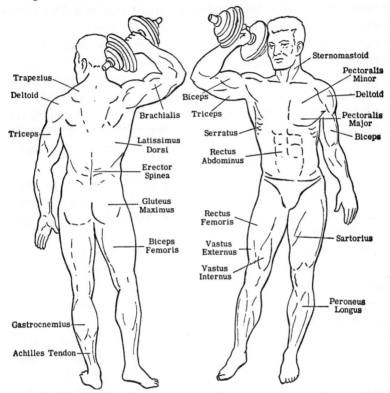

Figure 7. Musculature of the body (rear view).

Figure 8. Musculature of the body (front view).

point" * is reached, in which it seems impossible to add either repetitions or weight, it is advisable to approach the exercise routine differently, and it is often a good idea to lay off weight training a week or two before beginning a new approach.

One means of getting past a sticking point is to return to the

---

* "Sticking point": when a weight trainer is unable to add a single repetition, or unable to perform the same number of repetitions with more weight.

same exercises and repeat each one, two, or three times, working up from a lesser poundage. A man, pressing 150 pounds ten times and unable to progress, could begin by pressing 130 pounds eight times, then press 150 five times and 160 three times. This can be carried even further, to press 170 pounds twice and 180 or 190 pounds three to five single times. After a week at these poundages, an attempt should be made to handle 5 pounds more all along the line. The same system can be used, in squatting, by the man stuck at fifteen repetitions with 200 pounds. He could start (actually warm up) with 180 pounds for eight or ten repetitions, then go to 200 pounds for five squats, 220 pounds for five squats, 240 for three, and 250 for three. Repeating an exercise is called doing it in "sets."

Another means of working past the sticking point is to select a poundage slightly below that at which the exerciser is stuck and repeat the exercise ten repetitions three times. (Ten, ten, and ten.) This is another form of "sets."

Still another method is similar to that of the competitive weight lifter and involves the selection of a *heavier* weight, cutting the repetitions to five. This is repeated two or three times (sets) and then cut to three repetitions for one or two sets with an even heavier poundage.

It has been found that better results are gained from weight training if the exercise is not practiced daily. Time is needed for the building of muscles and if the exercise periods follow too closely, one after another, the time may not be sufficient. For the person who is underweight or weak, it is very important that no physical activity of any consequence be undertaken on the "off" days. For a person of normal health and strength, however, other activities on non-weight training days should have no adverse effect. A person trying to lose weight should exercise five or six days a week, but moderating the weight and increasing repetitions on the "off" days. It is advisable for everyone, of course, to have one or two days each week in which there is no vigorous activity.

All of the following barbell exercises can be practiced with dumbbells if barbells are not available.

The basic exercises

1. Warm-up. In any vigorous activity, it is customary to warm up the muscles before the actual exercise. Resistance exercise with barbells is no exception, and there are several good methods of warming up with a single exercise. One is to work the muscles in stages, as follows: Stand close to a barbell that is well within your strength ability to handle in any exercise. By lowering the hips, grasp the barbell with palms toward the legs at shoulder width. Maintain a straight back while pulling the weight up, and straighten fully and lean back slightly with the weight hanging across the thighs; lower the barbell to the floor and repeat three to five counts. Without setting the weight down, increase the action to the extent of pulling the barbell fully to the chest, but do not lift it overhead. Lower it again to a point below the knees and repeat the pull to the chest three to five times. Then, with the weight at the chest, push it overhead three to five times. This three-stage warm-up with a total of nine to fifteen actual movements will serve to activate all the muscles of the body.

Remember to maintain a straight back at all times when pulling weights up from the floor.

A simpler warm-up movement is to grasp the barbell (loaded to a moderate poundage according to the individual's ability), pull it from the floor to the chest and push it overhead, then lower all the way to the floor and repeat ten times.

Still another movement suitable for warming up the muscles is to grasp a barbell and pull it all the way from the floor to arms' length overhead ten repetitions.

2. Curl. An exercise which develops the biceps and allied arm and forearm muscles is the curl, which is performed as follows: The barbell is grasped with palms *away* from the legs and raised to a position across the thighs as the exerciser stands erect. Then it is raised to the chest (sternum) by flexing the arms (folding the forearms against the upper arms), the barbell moving in an arc as the elbows remain at the sides. (*See* Figure 9.) The exerciser should stand straight as possible throughout and endeavor to limit the action to the arms. (Eight to twelve repetitions.)

Figure 9. Curl.   *Figure 10. Press.*

This exercise can also be practiced starting with palms toward the legs. This variation, called the reverse curl, affects the forearms more strongly and less weight can be used.

3. *Press.* For general development of the shoulders and triceps of the arms, the following exercise is unexcelled: Grasp the barbell with palms toward the legs and pull it to the upper chest (remembering to go for the weight with back straight, by lowering the hips). Then push it to fully locked arms overhead, lower to the chest, and repeat the overhead lift. The exerciser should stand straight throughout the performance of this exercise, leaning back only slightly to get the barbell past the face. (*See* Figure 10.)

For the regular press, as described, the barbell should be held with a shoulder-width hand spacing. A valuable variation of this exercise, affecting the same muscles, but slightly differently, is to use a somewhat wider hand spacing and perform the presses from behind the neck. In pressing behind the neck, the barbell should be lowered all the way until it touches the shoulders. (Eight to twelve repetitions.)

4. Rowing. For development of the upper back muscles (and the arms), the following exercise is performed: With legs straight or very slightly bent, the exerciser leans forward and allows the barbell to hang just off the floor (palms of the hands toward the legs). The position is one with the body parallel to the horizon, bending forward from the hips. Without any motion of the legs or body, the barbell is pulled up to touch the chest at the bottom of the pectoral muscles. Then it is lowered and the movement repeated for the desired number of counts. (*See* Figure 11.) To eliminate body motion and be sure that the

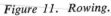

Figure 11. Rowing.   *Figure 12. Squat.*

upper back and arms are doing the work, it is a good idea to place the forehead against the top of the back of a chair, or something of similar height. (Eight to twelve repetitions.)

5. Squat. No exercise can match full knee bends with a

barbell on the shoulders for powerful thighs and hips. The barbell is placed on the shoulders at the back of the neck. The
exerciser can lift it there himself as though pressing, or it can
be placed across the shoulders by training partners, or it can be
lifted from shoulder-high stands. The heels can be raised slightly
on a board one or two inches thick for comfort. Keeping the
back straight and chest high, the exerciser lowers into a full
squat and rises, repeating for the desired number of counts.

A variation of this exercise is to practice squats with a barbell
while maintaining an on-toes position, as in doing free-hand
calisthenic knee bends. (*See* Figure 12.) Squatting on toes helps
develop balance as well as strength, and is valuable when only
comparatively light weights are available, being more difficult
than the flat-footed variety with a given weight.

When squatting on toes, the feet should be kept close together,
with toes turned out somewhat. When squatting flat-footed (with
or without the heels elevated), any comfortable stance is advised.
Usually the most comfortable position will be to place the heels
at approximately shoulder width, with the toes pointing slightly
outward. (Ten to fifteen repetitions.)

6. *Pullover.* The straight-arm pullover is one which should
be practiced with a light weight in order that proper emphasis
can be placed on correct breathing for chest expansion. It is a
good idea to practice pullovers immediately after a vigorous
movement like the squat, which will have created a natural need
for deep breathing.

Lying supine, the barbell is grasped at shoulder width with
arms stretched fully over (behind) the head. After inhaling fully
it is pulled over to a position directly above the chest, exhaling as
the weight rises in an arc. It is then lowered to the starting position with accompanying full inhalation as it is lowered. (*See*
Figure 13.) The raising and lowering of the barbell, accompanied by exhalation and inhalation, is continued for the desired
number of counts. No attempt should be made to handle heavy
weights in this exercise and the arms should remain rigid. In

almost every case, the weight of the bar alone will be sufficient
at the start. Ten to fifteen repetitions should be performed, with
a weight that is comfortable to use throughout the exercise.

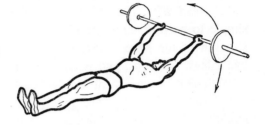

*Figure 13. Straight-arm
      pullover.*

7. *Rise-on-toes.* The calf muscles are dense and hard-to-
develop because of the action they receive in walking, even in
the case of the most sedentary person. To develop greater
strength and size, it is necessary to work this muscle from full
extension to full contraction against heavy resistance. The barbell is placed across the shoulders at the back of the neck, and
the toes and balls of the feet are elevated on a 2-inch board, or
higher, to allow the heels to extend below the level of support
and stretch the muscles. The exerciser then rises fully on the
toes, lowers, and repeats for the desired number of counts. (*See*
Figure 14.)

Figure 14. Rise-on-toes.

It is a good system to work the calves by placing the feet in three positions; toes pointing in, out, and straight ahead. Ten to fifteen repetitions should be performed in each position, since the calves need more work than other portions of the body.

8. Dead lift. The dead lift, while it sounds ominous, is simple to perform and one of the best exercises to develop the strength of the lower back. It also strengthens the grip, upper back, legs, and hips, and is an excellent test of strength.

With feet spaced comfortably apart, bend the knees, lower the hips, and lean forward to grasp the barbell. Then simply straighten fully until the barbell is resting across the thighs with the body erect and shoulders back. (*See* Figure 15.) Lower and repeat. To make it easier to hold the barbell until the repetitions are completed, the hands may be reversed, one palm toward the legs and the other away. (Eight to twelve repetitions.)

Figure 15. Dead lift.   *Figure 16. Upright rowing.*

9. Upright rowing. An exercise to develop the trapezius, deltoids, and allied upper back muscles, as well as the arms, is performed as follows: Hold a barbell (palms toward the body). with a narrow hand spacing, at the hang position across the thighs. Then, keeping elbows higher than the barbell throughout the movement, pull it up along the abdomen and chest to the throat or chin. (*See* Figure 16.) The legs and body should remain straight throughout the exercise. The entire action is the pull from hang position to the throat, working from eight to twelve repetitions.

10. Press on bench. To develop the muscles of the chest, as well as the triceps of the arms and the deltoids, one of the best exercises is to press a barbell from a point on the pectorals to locked arms over the chest while lying supine. (*See* Figure 17.) The hands should be placed slightly wider than the breadth of the shoulders. Arm strength will be affected more if the elbows are kept close to the sides; the pectorals will be developed more if the elbows are held wide.

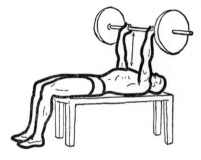

Figure 17. Press on bench.

To place the barbell in position, it can be lifted to a position at the top of the thighs while the exerciser seats himself at the end of the bench and lies down. He then tosses the barbell back on the chest by forcibly bridging up and back with a leg thrust, keeping shoulders in place on the bench. If training partners are present, they can hand the barbell to the exerciser (in which case more weight can be handled with greater comfort and safety). The exercise can also be practiced lying supine on the floor or a mat if no sturdy bench is available. (Eight to twelve repetitions.)

11. Bent-arm lateral raise, lying. A combined chest-expanding and pectoral-developing exercise is performed as follows: The exerciser grasps a pair of dumbbells and lies supine on a bench. With arms slightly bent and held rigid, the weights are lowered, in arcs to each side, from a point directly over the chest. The lowering to full stretch of the pectoral muscles is accompanied by forceful inhalation. The dumbbells are then returned to the starting point in the same arc, with exhalation. (*See* Figure 18.) (Eight to twelve repetitions is recommended, but weight and repetition increases will be more gradual in a leverage exercise of this type.)

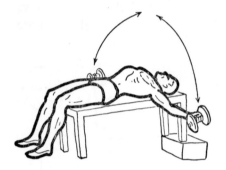

Figure 18. Bent-arm lateral raise, lying.

12. Lateral raise, standing. For direct development of the deltoid muscles of the shoulders, the exerciser should stand in a position of attention with dumbbells held at the sides, arms straight. Keeping the arms straight and knuckles up, the dumbbells are raised directly to the sides in a full semicircular arc until they are fully overhead. (*See* Figure 19.) The arms should be kept rigid throughout. It will be found necessary to rotate the hands to bring the dumbbells fully overhead, but this rotation should be avoided as much as possible, which means that the knuckles should be pointing up as far along in the arc as possible. The knuckles should remain up until the hands have passed the height of the ears in every case. (Eight to twelve repetitions.)

The abdominal muscles

The muscles of the trunk are involved in nearly every exercise described, but it is advisable to include either the sit-up or leg-raise exercise in order to work the muscles of the abdomen directly. These can be made progressively more difficult by holding weight behind the head in the sit-up, or attaching weight to the feet in the leg-raise. (*See* Figure 20.) Another means of making these exercises harder, and therefore more effective, is to work up an incline, gradually increasing the angle. For ordinary purposes of strengthening and conditioning the mid-section, the sit-up and leg-raise exercises should be practiced from ten to fifteen or twenty repetitions, adding weight when the higher number is reached.

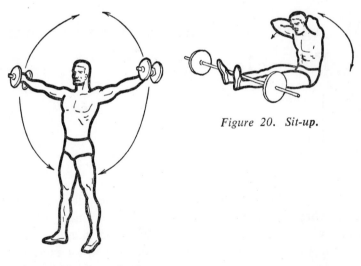

Figure 20. Sit-up.

Figure 19. Lateral raise, standing.

Chapter 6

Weight Training Variation Exercises

IN addition to the basic exercises described in the preceding chapter, there are many good weight training movements which will aid in development of the same muscles, but in a different manner. They are worth including in an exercise program occasionally, if only to relieve boredom. The following descriptions are of the better barbell/dumbbell exercise variations.

A short bar (dumbbell bar length of about 18 inches) is loaded at the center, without collars. This is called a "swingbell." The exerciser sits on a bench or stool and grasps the swingbell with palms away from himself, holding it outside of the plates so the hands keep the weights in place. (*See* Figure 21.) Leaning forward and keeping the elbows stationary by bracing them between the legs, he curls the weight to the chest, lowers to full extension, and repeats for the desired number of repetitions (ordinarily eight to twelve).

A similar exercise can be practiced one arm at a time, using a regular dumbbell and bracing the exercising arm against the thigh. In this method, the arms must be exercised alternately. (*See* Figure 22.)

Figure 21. "Swing-bell" curling.   *Figure 22. Curling with one dumbbell.*   *Figure 23. Curling with two dumbbells.*

Curling with two dumbbells can be practiced while seated, allowing the weights to carry well back to the sides to full elbow lock before bringing them back to the shoulders by flexing the arms. The dumbbells are pointed front and back during most of the action, but the palms are turned up just as they reach the shoulders. This exercise can also be practiced standing, but sitting down helps prevent body sway, which takes the work away from the flexors. (*See* Figure 23.) The two dumbbells can be curled alternately, one being raised as the other is lowered, for more variety.

For the forearm flexors and wrists

To strengthen the wrists and forearms, a "wrist curl" movement is done as follows: Seated on a bench or stool, the exerciser grasps a barbell with palms up, supporting his forearms to the wrists on his thighs. He then works his hand through the fullest possible range of movement, allowing the barbell to roll down in his fingers and then bringing it up as high as the mobility of his wrist will permit. (*See* Figure 24.)

Figure 24. Wrist curl.   *Figure 25. Wrist curl with dumbbell weighted at one end.*   *Figure 26. Raise from behind the neck.*

The same exercise can be performed with the palms down.

Another forearm exercise is practiced standing, by holding a dumbbell loaded *at one end only* by the unloaded end, with the weighted end extending forward from the thumb end of the hand. The weighted end is then raised and lowered through the full range of wrist action, the forearm remaining stationary at the side throughout. (*See* Figure 25.)

The same exercise can be performed with the weighted end of the dumbbell extending backward.

For the arm extensors

Weakness in the straightening muscles of the arms can be overcome by working them over the full range of extension and contraction while immobilizing the deltoids as much as possible. One exercise, which acts directly on the triceps, is the raising of a barbell (or swingbell) from behind the neck to fully locked arms overhead. (*See* Figure 26.) The elbows should be kept as stationary as possible, pointing straight up, throughout the exercise.

The same exercise can be practiced, one arm at a time, with a dumbbell. This is an exercise that can be used to strengthen an elbow weakened by injury in a sports activity, like javelin-throwing. In such use, however, the arm should be warmed up with dumbbell (or barbell) pressing before the extension movement is used.

A similar extension movement can be done while lying supine, using a barbell or dumbbells. The exerciser holds the weight at arms' length over the chest and then lowers it to touch above and behind the head by bending the arms, keeping the elbows up. The movement is completed by returning the weight in an arc to its starting point. It is possible to use dumbbells, one in each hand, by lowering one to each side of the head.

For the shoulders (deltoid muscles)

A man can develop large, strong deltoid muscles by the presses and lateral raises described previously, but for the sake of variety, and the benefit derived from working the muscles from the "different angle," the following exercises are valuable.

For the anterior deltoids, alternate straight-arm forward raises are performed with dumbbells, lowering one as the other is raised. The weights move from in front of the thighs, in arcs, to an overhead position. (*See* Figure 27.)

For the posterior deltoids, simultaneous raises are performed while leaning forward at a right angle from the hips, lifting the dumbbells directly to the sides as high as possible (with arms straight). (*See* Figure 28.) This exercise is called the "lateral raise, leaning."

A complete arm and shoulder exercise can be done in one compound movement by curling two dumbbells, then pressing them overhead, and lowering to the shoulders before repeating the curl. Pressing dumbbells will affect the deltoids more if they are held wide and pointed to the sides at the shoulders. If the handles are pointed front and back, and the weights are pressed vertically from on top of the deltoids, the triceps will receive relatively more action.

For the chest

The chest muscles will be developed by the supine press and supine dumbbell raises described previously, but it is possible to work them more completely by using different angles.

By slanting the exercise bench more nearly toward the vertical (raising the head end), pressing from the chest works the upper section of the pectorals more (and also the anterior deltoids). When this exercise is done with dumbbells, pointing them to the sides and holding the elbows wide of the body, it is possible to give the pectorals (and rib box) more stretch, as well as to contract the pectorals more completely by bringing the weights together as the arms are straightened over the chest. (*See* Figure 29.)

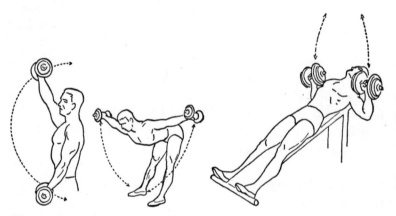

Figure 27. Alternate straight - arm forward raises.

Figure 28. Lateral raise, leaning.

Figure 29. Press on slanting bench.

The lower portion of the pectorals can be developed by raising the foot end of the bench, or by practicing dips on parallel bars with a dumbbell or plate tied to the belt.

To increase the size of the rib box while performing chest exercises, the exerciser should inhale fully as the weight is lowered, exhale as it is raised. A dumbbell pullover can be done alternately, starting with both weights over the chest, arms straight. The right arm is lowered behind the head and the left to the left thigh, with inhalation. Then the right arm is pulled over to the right thigh and the left arm back behind the head. Full exhalation should be reached as the weights pass each other over the chest.

For the upper back

The latissimus dorsi and allied muscles, which pull the arms down and back, will respond readily to the basic rowing and pullover exercises. For additional work, chinning (touching the chest or the back of the neck to the bar) can be employed as a weight training exercise by attaching weights to the belt.

A one-arm rowing motion can also be practiced effectively with a heavy dumbbell. In this, the exerciser leans forward and braces his hand on an object that will bring his back to a horizontal level. He then pulls the dumbbell up, and to the side, as far as possible. (*See* Figure 30.)

A bent-arm pullover, lying supine, will also work these muscles, and will help enlarge the rib box as well. The exerciser places a barbell on the floor at the head end of a bench 16 to 18 inches high. Lying supine, with his head past the end of the bench and hanging down, he reaches back and grasps the barbell with a shoulder-width or narrower grip. Then, keeping the arms at the same angle, he pulls the weight in an arc to the chest, lowers, and repeats. Conscious inhalation while lowering the weight, exhalation while pulling over, is recommended. Considerably more weight can be used in this manner than in the pullover with arms straight.

The trapezius and allied muscles will respond to all exercises in which the barbell is pulled above the hang position in front of the thighs. A direct trapezius exercise, however, is to hold a weight at the hang position and simply shrug the shoulders as high as possible. Rotating the shoulders in a circular motion while shrugging, first forward and then backward, will add to the effectiveness of the exercise. This is a movement in which surprisingly heavy weights can be handled, so it may be necessary to alternate the grip of the hands, as in dead lifting.

For the lower back and hips

All forms of lifting from the floor, as well as squatting exercises, work the lower back and hips, but there are two fine exercises which will help overcome weakness in this part of the body with direct action. The first is to perform the dead weight lift with legs straight, in what amounts to a toe-touching exercise while holding a barbell. Additional stretch can be provided by standing on a box or bench so the bar can actually be touched to the insteps. The second exercise is very similar, a forward bend with a barbell held on the shoulders behind the neck. In both movements, the exerciser should move smoothly, and be cautious in his selection of weights, in order to avoid strain and resulting soreness. While dead lifting with legs straight, a good workout can be obtained by doing ten repetitions with no more than body weight, although it is possible to handle much more when the back has been conditioned to the work. In the forward bend (often called the "good morning exercise" because it looks like a polite bow), considerably less weight can be used.

Another lower back exercise is performed prone, with the legs supported to the hips and an assistant holding down the feet. The exerciser holds a light weight behind his head and alternately arches up as far as possible, then allows his head and torso to drop below the level of the bench. (*See* Figure 31.) The emphasis in this exercise is on complete contraction of the lower back muscles, or as much as is possible. This is called the back hyperextension.

With dumbbells, the lower back can be worked vigorously by swinging one or two weights from overhead all the way back between the legs and then overhead again. The knees are allowed to bend naturally and the arm(s) is kept straight, but not rigid, throughout the swing. If one dumbbell is used at a time, the non-lifting hand should rest on the thigh, just above the knee.

Still another hip (and to a lesser extent, lower back) exercise is performed while lying prone with weighted exercise sandals strapped to the feet. The exerciser works one leg (hip) at a time by raising the foot as high as possible by contraction of the buttock.

For the thighs (*extensors*)

The regular full squat exercise is the best single thigh developer, and it also works the hips and lower back to some extent; but there are a number of other fine leg-developing movements. One is to squat with the weight held at the chest, so that the leverage (keeping trunk erect) is thrown more on the extensor muscles close to the knees. Another means of placing the work lower on the thighs is to hold the barbell at the buttocks behind the body and squat with the heels raised at least two inches and feet close together. The body should be kept erect and the weight held in place throughout, for it is not the same exercise when the weight is allowed to hang free during the squat. This exercise, "the Hack lift," was named for George Hackenschmidt, who favored it. Hackenschmidt practiced it as a squat on toes, an even more difficult movement because of the balance involved.

The full knee bend with weight on shoulders can be done on toes, and this variation is especially valuable if heavy weights are not available. The feet should be placed together, with toes turned out, when squatting on toes (actually on the balls of the feet).

The leg extension movement described as an exercise for football players (Chapter 9) is another good one for the thighs, especially to strengthen the muscles around the knees.

Partial knee bends are a valuable strength builder, but require enough weights so the barbell can be loaded to from 300 to as much as 500 or 700 pounds. It is also necessary to have stands for the barbell which are nearly shoulder height. The weight is taken on the shoulders from the stands and the legs are bent and straightened a few inches. A partial bend exercise, called the Jefferson lift, can be practiced with the barbell suspended below the body. The exerciser straddles the weight and raises it from the floor until it is suspended just under the crotch, and then performs short-range knee bends.

For the thighs (flexors)

The flexing muscles at the rear of the thighs can be exercised standing, and lying supine, by attaching weights to the feet. Weighted sandals, available commercially, have holes through which dumbbell or barbell handles can be thrust for progression in weight resistance. Lying prone, preferably up an incline, both legs can be exercised together by curling the sandals and barbell from straight legs to touch the buttocks. (If the angle is steep, it may not be possible to touch the buttocks, but the legs should be curled up to fullest possible contraction.)

One leg at a time can be worked by attaching one sandal with a dumbbell and curling with the leg while standing on a box or bench. (See Figure 32.) Balance should be maintained by holding to a door frame or leaning against a wall. It is necessary to stand elevated from the floor to give the weight clearance.

(Note: There are many possible exercises of value which can be practiced with weighted iron sandals. The leg adductors can be strengthened by lying supine and working the legs in a scissors motion—from pointing vertically together to lateral extension and back together. A football or soccer player can develop strong kicking action with a single weight attached. The well-known inverted bicycling calisthenic movement can be made much more effective by the addition of a pair of five-pound sandals [or even more weight on dumbbell handles].)

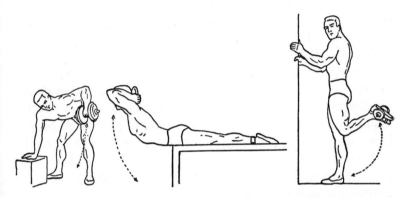

Figure 30. One-arm   Figure 31. Back   Figure 32. Leg curl.
     rowing.   hyperextension.

For the trunk

To develop the muscles of the sides, leaning from side to side with a light barbell across the shoulders, and with the legs straight, is effective.

Another side exercise is to hold a single dumbbell alongside the leg and place the other hand behind the head, then lean as far toward the weighted side as possible and finally return as far past the vertical as the contraction of the side muscles *opposite* the weight will permit.

The feet should be placed only 10 or 12 inches apart in these side exercises.

For the calves

To supplement the basic rise-on-toes, there are a number of variations. One is to work a single leg at a time, while holding a dumbbell on the side of the leg being exercised, holding a door frame or leaning against a wall for balance with the other hand.

With a barbell on the shoulders, or a dumbbell in each hand, the calves will receive vigorous work by vertical jumping, using as much calf spring and as little thigh power as possible. Because the calf muscles are so dense and "immune" to fatigue, these jumps can be repeated twenty to fifty times without stopping.

Carrying this action further, the regular straddle hop can be performed with a barbell on the shoulders (preferably padded at the center where it touches the body). Again the action should be directed as much as possible to the calves by limiting the amount of knee bending and by keeping the heels from coming into contact with the floor. Care must be taken in this exercise to keep the barbell from bouncing free of the shoulders at the back of the neck. It should be held low on the shoulders so the trapezius muscles can keep pressure from the spine.

For the neck

Additional vigorous work can be placed on the neck by carrying the wrestler's bridge (with weight on chest) further. Two possible variations are to bridge and press a barbell over the chest simultaneously, or to assume the bridge position and pullover a barbell to the chest with bent arms and then press it. Lifting while bridging provides the same type of violent action as wrestling so is a valuable conditioner for the wrestler. George Hackenschmidt, when a champion Greco-Roman wrestler, succeeded in pulling over and pressing a 311-pound barbell.

Various types of headgear, which are available commercially, can be used effectively to develop the neck muscles. Weight is attached to the headgear and suspended in front or in back of the exerciser while the head is moved forward, backward, and in rotation.

The back of the neck can be developed by suspending a weight in a loop formed by a folded towel and gripping the towel firmly well back in the teeth. While holding the weight suspended by jaw strength, leaning forward with hands above knees, the head is moved backward and forward.

Use of variation exercises

When progress slows in the basic exercises, it is often a result of boredom with practicing the same exercises over a period of time as well as the fact that the muscles are reaching a normal strength and size. To continue progress, it is a good idea to vary the weight training program by either substituting variation exercises, or by using them in addition to the twelve basic movements.

An example of substitution is as follows:

Basic	Variation I	Variation II
Warm-up	Warm-up	Warm-up
Curl	Reverse curl	Swingbell curl, seated
Press	Press behind neck	Triceps extension
Rowing	Chin behind neck	Bent-arm pullover
Squat	Squat, weight in front	Hack squat
Pullover	Pullover	Alternate pullover
Rise-on-toes	One-leg rise-on-toes	Straddle hop
Dead lift	Stiff-legged dead lift	Back hyperextension
Upright rowing	Shrug with barbell	Repetition clean
Press on bench	Dumbbell press on incline	Press on bench
Bent-arm lateral raise	Dips on parallel bars	Alternate pullover
Lateral raise, standing	Alternate forward raise	Lateral raise, leaning
Sit-up	Leg raise	Side bend

As can be seen, an endless variety is possible by shuffling the weight training exercises. It is a workable plan to follow a different routine each of the three training days of the week. If only one or two exercises are changed, it will relieve monotony. Most experienced weight trainers change the entire routine every few weeks, following the new schedule regularly until another "sticking point" is reached. It is often a good idea to eliminate weight training entirely for a week when changing schedules.

If only dumbbells are available, a complete routine can be planned as follows:

> Warm-up clean and press.
> Curl, starting with thumbs up.
> Alternate press.
> Rowing, one arm at a time.
> Squat, holding dumbbells at shoulders or at sides.
> Pullover.
> Vertical jumps, dumbbells at side.
> Stiff-legged dead lift.
> Shrugs, holding dumbbells.
> Supine press, slight incline.
> Bent-arm lateral raise.
> Lateral raise, standing.
> Sit-up, dumbbell behind head.

For the advanced weight trainer already performing sets in his training, adding variation movements to the routine can add to the severity or provide a means of specializing on body parts that the exerciser believes need more development. An example of a complete routine, such as the "Mr. America" contestant often uses, is as follows:

Warm-up.
Barbell press—Two sets, ten repetitions; eight reps, four reps.
  (Weight increased after each set.)
Lateral raise—Two sets, ten-fifteen repetitions.
Alternate forward raise—Two sets, ten-fifteen repetitions, each arm.
Upright rowing—Two sets, ten-fifteen repetitions.
Rowing exercise—Four-five sets, ten-twelve repetitions.
Leg curl—Four sets, ten-fifteen repetitions.
Leg extension—Three sets, ten-fifteen repetitions.
Squat—Fifteen repetitions.
Pullover—Fifteen-twenty repetitions with light dumbbells.
Stiff-legged dead lift—Two sets, ten repetitions.
Sit-ups—Four sets of fifty repetitions on incline, no weight.
Rise-on-toes—Five sets, twenty repetitions.
Barbell curl—Two sets, ten reps; two sets, eight reps.
  (Weight increased after each set.)
One-arm dumbbell curl—Two sets, fifteen repetitions.
  (Completing a set with each arm before repeating.)
Triceps extension, standing—Four sets, fifteen-twenty-five repetitions.

The foregoing is the actual schedule of exercises followed by Jim Park, a "Mr. America" contest winner who was preparing for the international "Mr. Universe" contest, which he won. Note that considerable planning went into this program. The first four exercises mainly work the deltoids. The only latissimus dorsi exercise is next, followed by three thigh exercises. The squats were placed third in the group, to be followed by the pullover breathing exercises. After this, single exercises were included for the lower back, abdominal muscles, and the calves. The final three exercises were aimed directly at the arm flexors and extensors. In the entire routine, the arms and shoulders, most "showy" in best-developed-man contests, received the most attention, but note that at least one exercise was included for each main body part to insure an all-around workout. All the exercises were practiced in more sets and repetitions than usual because Park was striving for extreme muscular definition * as well as development. Note the total of two hundred sit-ups for the mid-section.

Naturally strong, and with a superb physique by ordinary standards at his normal weight of 195 pounds (at 69½ inches height), Park wore himself down to a pound or two over 180 in order to meet the standards in vogue among muscle enthusiasts, and at the same time, maintained huge arm and shoulder development. This was purely a calculated effort on Park's part, for he preferred a heavier workout with less repetitions. When not preparing for a closely-approaching physique contest, Park preferred to work up to poundages like 265 in the press and 500 or more in the dead lift. When trained down for sharp muscularity, he was unable to handle his ordinary limit poundages. Unlike many of his contemporaries in best-developed-man competition, Park preferred a day tramping the mountains, hunting game in season, to doing sets of sit-ups for "definition."

While not recommended as a conditioning program, because

---

* Muscular definition: a finely trained condition in which the muscles are visible through the skin.

of its severity, the training program used by Park does show how exercises can be put together purposefully to achieve specific results. Such planning to separate closely related exercises as those for the arms and deltoids enables a man to give more work to each than if they followed in order.

Specialization programs can be set up for more practical purposes than to achieve a striking muscular appearance, however, and a weight building routine serves as an example. The following program could be used during the winter months to build up a promising football player with all the needed qualities except size and strength. It can also be used to build up a person who is simply weak and underweight:

Warm-up.
Curl—Ten repetitions.
Press—Ten repetitions.
Rowing exercise—Three sets, ten repetitions.
Supine press—Three sets, ten repetitions.
Full squat—Fifteen reps., ten reps., eight repetitions.
   (Ten-pound weight increase after each set of squats followed by ten repetitions in the deep-breathing pullover using a light weight.)

This is not a properly balanced program for an average person, of course, and would result in overdevelopment of the thighs, pectorals, and upper back at the expense of other muscles. For an underweight person, however, it serves the purpose of adding weight and strength without undue fatigue. After results have been achieved with this program, the exerciser could change to a routine based on the twelve fundamental exercises (or the football conditioning routine). An underweight person should deliberately be as "lazy" as possible until the condition has been overcome, and should eat a fully nourishing diet while getting at least eight hours sleep nightly. It must be emphasized that the foregoing is *not* recommended as a permanent training program, for after two or three months it would not be developing athletic ability or an attractive physique. It might become, in time, detrimental to the individual's health and personality because of unbalanced physical development. The fact remains that a person who makes a permanent habit of "laziness" and his life's work the development of large chest and thighs is not always well-received in society.

One of the best ways to include variation exercises in a training program is to include them in addition to the basic movements, when the muscles no longer respond sufficiently to the fundamental program. An example of this use is as follows:

Warm-up
Curl
    Reverse curl
    Swingbell curl, seated
Press
    Press behind neck
    Triceps extension
Rowing
    Chin behind neck
    Bent-arm pullover
Squat (followed by pullover)
    Leg extension
    Leg curl

Rise-on-toes
    Vertical jumping
Dead lift
    Back hyperextension
Upright rowing
    Shoulder shrug
Press on bench
    Dumbbell press on incline
Bent-arm lateral raise, lying
Lateral raise, standing
    Alternate forward raise
Sit-up
    Side bend

All these exercises can be practiced progressively from eight to twelve (or ten to fifteen) repetitions, or can be practiced with heavy weights for five to eight repetitions in the basic movements, followed by twelve to fifteen in the variations. Using this latter system, the basic exercises would be practiced with heavy weights, and lighter poundages used for the variations.

Another means of adding variety to the weight training routine is to substitute three or more of the variation movements for three to six workouts, after which another group can be substituted, returning to the basic movements in the original three (or more). In this way, a complete training program for the entire body can be made "different" every two weeks.

All the possible combinations of exercises are not listed, for any individual should be able to devise suitable programs according to needs and personal aims from the information given. The variation exercises should follow the repetitions and sets suggested in the chapter on basic exercise.

A "keep fit" routine

One more use of exercises not discussed elsewhere is a "keep fit" routine, which can be practiced in a mimimum of time. One of the best exercises in this category is the warm-up movement involving complete cleans and presses, except that more weight should be used than when the exercise is merely a warm-up. Another very stimulating movement is to place a weight on the shoulders and perform deep knee bends with a press from behind neck after each squat. These two exercises, using as much weight as possible for ten or twelve repetitions each, will serve to keep a man's muscles toned up if practiced daily. This minimum amount of exercise is valuable if no overweight problem exists. The exercises can be done in sets of three if time permits. A man can maintain above-average strength and condition by doing these exercises ten repetitions with from 75 to 100 pounds. For the man with more time available, a slightly more involved routine would include clean and press, ten repetitions; full squat, fifteen repetitions; pullover, fifteen repetitions; sit-up or leg-raise, thirty repetitions; clean and press, ten repetitions. Anyone able to do the clean and press, and squat exercises with 100 pounds, can consider himself above average in strength. If available, however, the squat should be done with more weight than the clean and press.

References

(*I*) BOOKS

(*1*) Hoffman, Bob, *Simplified System of Barbell Training*. York, Pa.: York Barbell Company.
(*2*) Murray, Al, *Basic Weight Training*. London: George Grose Ltd., 1954.
(*3*) Murray, Jim, *Weight Lifting and Progressive Resistance Exercise*. New York: A. S. Barnes and Company, 1954.
(*4*) Paschall, Harry B., *The Bosco System of Progressive Physical Training*. Columbus, Ohio: published by the author, 1954.
(*5*) ———, *Development of Strength*. London: Vigour Press Ltd.
(*6*) ———, *Muscle Moulding*. London: Vigour Press Ltd.

Part IV

Chapter 7

For the Instructor and Coach

THE use of weight training exercises to assist athletes specializing in sports other than lifting, has, in recent years, gained considerable popularity. In the United States, this supplementary weight training has often been undertaken by the individual athlete, with little supervision or instruction. Colleges that are notable exceptions are the State University of Iowa and the University of Arizona. Abroad, especially in England, Australia, and Russia, specified organized weight training programs have been used successfully. Australian coaches Harry Hopman (tennis) and Percy Cerutty (track and field) have worked with

Frank Findlay, an experienced weight training instructor, who prescribes and instructs in the performance of exercise to correct specific individual weaknesses. The program showed results in improving the play of Frank Sedgman and the running of John Landy. Findlay, the Australian trainer, picked up valuable pointers on visits to the United States where he spent time with such men as Olympic weight lifting coach Bob Hoffman and team trainer Ray Van Cleef. It is ironic that the methods used by American lifting coaches gained ready acceptance abroad while they had been rejected for years by the majority of U.S. physical educators and coaches without being investigated.

Equipment for weight training

The basic equipment for weight training is a barbell and a pair of dumbbells. The barbell is simply a steel bar 4 to 6 feet long, the dumbbells, a pair of short bells 12 to 18 inches long. Both have "collars" that are held to the bar (usually by screws) to keep the weights in place at the ends, and the disc-shaped weights with holes in the centers to fit snugly on the bars. In addition it is advisable to have foot weights. These are best described as weighted sandals with holes for the insertion of two short bars or a single longer bar for additional weight. A sturdy bench, 12 to 16 inches wide and 4 to 6 feet long, is needed for some exercises which are done lying supine. The bench should be at least 16 inches high. Because barbells and dumbbells are hard on polished gymnasium floors, they should be set on mats or in rugged wooden racks. It is a good idea to have mats placed about 26 inches apart on the floor, so that the weights can be set on padding while the exerciser stands between the pads on solid floor.

Weight training equipment can be purchased in almost any sporting goods store, or from a number of mail-order companies. A coach or instructor buying in any quantity can expect a discount, and should do some "shopping" before he buys. Prices will be lower in purchasing direct from a mail-order dealer and addresses of barbell-dumbbell firms can be found in "physical culture magazines" and other publications slanted primarily toward the male reader. The purchaser should take into consideration the location of the manufacturer, since he will be expected to pay the freight on the weighty equipment.

In some cases, it may be possible to purchase equipment direct from a foundry and steel producer. Many foundries are equipped to cast weights in 25, 10, 5, 2½, and other poundages. Bars can be cut to length in machine shops and equipped with collars at the same time.

Use of weight training exercises in groups

In order to provide weight training exercises for a group of any size, such as a class in physical education, it will be necessary to have several adjustable barbells available. A group of twenty-four men, for example, could be divided into six units of four men each and get a full workout in an hour, by using six barbells. The men should be divided into units of approximately equal strength, to make possible minimum changing of weights as the men take their turns.

In the group comprised of the four weakest men in the class, the barbell could be loaded to a weight of 25 pounds for the warm-up and curl exercises. Since most men can handle more weight in the press and rowing exercise, the last man in line would add 2½ or 5-pound weights to the bar after completing his curls. At the opposite end of the gym, the strongest members of the class can be adding poundage from 90 to 120 on the barbell.

The selection of exercising poundages is largely a matter of common sense and trials. In early workouts, it is wise to err toward lighter weights than the exercisers can handle, in order to avoid unnecessary muscular soreness before the muscles become accustomed to the vigorous activity. Also, it is easier to learn the movements of the exercises when all-out effort is not involved in moving the weight.

Suggested trial weights for arm exercises (curl, press, rowing, etc.) are 25 to 50 pounds. For the legs (squat, rise-on-toes), more weight can be used at the start and 40 to 75 pounds is suggested. In the dead lift, it should be possible to learn the exercise with 75 to 100 pounds. The abdominal exercises (sit-up and leg-raise) can be begun with no weight at all for additional resistance. When dumbbells are used, they should weigh 5 to 10 pounds until the exerciser learns how much he can handle.

There is *little danger of strain* in any of the exercises. The method of performance should be explained and demonstrated. When the exercise is done properly there is no reason why there should be any more danger of strain than in other sports. In the case of a man who is abnormally weak, due to recovery from an injury or illness, exercise should be limited at the start. Not only should the weight be held down, but repetitions should be kept at five-eight and only a few exercises should be practiced. An unusual case such as this can be handled by the use of supine presses and dead lifts alone at first, using only the steel bar without weights. As soon as two sets of eight repetitions become easy, the weight should be increased by 5 pounds in these two movements and additional exercises used. The curl and leg extension are recommended. After this the weights and repetitions are gradually increased, first repetitions from five to eight and then the weight. As strength increases, more exercises are included until the basic group is used.

The person of average strength and condition will find no such problem. He will be able to proceed without strain, for as long as more than five repetitions are possible, fatigue will stop the movement before injury can occur.

As is the case in many other physical activities, such as running, most men will not "push themselves" sufficiently. Once the group has begun to show progress, the instructor should encourage weight increases whenever possible, and either coax or exhort, depending on the individual's temperament, the student to work for the extra repetition. It should be remembered that the body's warning system is often overly efficient when it comes to fatigue. We are seldom as tired or as fully extended as we think we are.

Points for emphasis by instructors

Correct lifting position is one of the most valuable bits of knowledge a student can derive from a course in weight lifting exercise. The instructor should emphasize at all times the importance of lifting any heavy object with the body placed as follows: Feet on the same line, hips lowered, head up, and back straight. In lifting *anything* heavy, be it a barbell, piece of furniture, or an opponent in a wrestling match, this is the most efficient body position. It is the position least likely to result in strain of either the back or abdomen. It is the position in which the largest and strongest muscles of the body, those of the legs and back, can be brought into play.

When "cleaning"—lifting a barbell from the floor to the chest in a single pull—the start should always be made as described above. In addition to keeping a straight back, and going for the weight by lowering the hips, the lifter should stand as close to the barbell (or object) as comfortably possible. As his hands grasp the barbell, his shins should actually be brushing the bar. The initial pull when cleaning is made by straightening the legs. As the barbell reaches knee height, the coordinated pull of the entire back and arms speeds its passage to the upper chest. Remember, when the pull is started by the legs, the barbell is, in effect, *lighter* when the weaker arm muscles take over, because of the momentum already imparted to it.

Probably the most important weight training exercises—those which should appear in some form in every program—are the clean to the shoulders, the press overhead, and the squat with barbell on shoulders. No form of exercise compares with lifting a barbell (and/or dumbbells) for development of leg strength, back strength, and the combined strength of arms and shoulders. The squat develops the legs, the clean the back, and the press the arms and shoulders. (*See* Figure 33.) The results produced

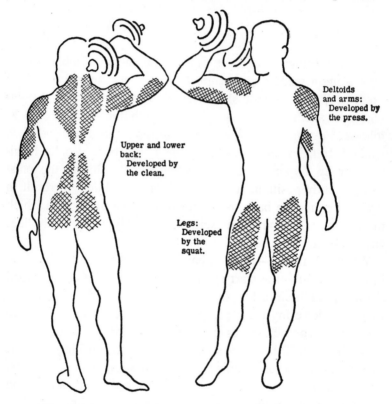

Upper and lower
back:
  Developed by
  the clean.

Deltoids
and arms:
  Developed by
  the press.

Legs:
  Developed
  by the
  squat.

Figure 33. Muscles developed by clean, press, and squat.

by these weight training movements make their use worth trying by any athlete or individual striving to attain maximum physical efficiency. (These exercises are also discussed at the end of the track and field chapter.)

Grading a weight training class

There are a number of possible approaches to grading a class in weight training. One is for the instructor to subjectively mark his pupils according to progress and application to the program. Over a half school year of weight training, a student who progressed from pressing 50 pounds ten times to pressing 95 pounds ten times has improved 90 per cent in strength (although some of the improvement must be credited to "learning" to exert the muscles efficiently in the exercises). Such improvement could be graded A or B, depending on the student's attitude, etc. A 50 per cent improvement would rate C for an average student, but might be graded higher or lower for students with below or above average physical development to start. For a passing grade, any student should be able to make a 25 per cent improvement in the majority of standard exercises. This would only involve an increase from 50 to 62½ pounds in the press exercise.

It should be taken into consideration that a student who has practiced weight training on his own initiative will probably *not be able to progress as rapidly as a complete newcomer*. As long as the experienced weight trainer continues to apply himself conscientiously, and does make improvement, there is no reason not to give him a high grade.

Arbitrary standards for "pass" or "fail" grades can be set up. A single lift in the press of 10 per cent less than body weight is attainable for any student but the abnormally sub-par, but may not be reached in a half-year semester. This would be comparable to a full knee bend with a barbell equal to body weight, and it would be advisable to select a certain standard of attainment in basic exercises for each part of the body. This could require a single lift performance or any given number of repetitions up to ten. A year's experiment with a weight training program, grading the first year subjectively, would provide a record of gains which could be averaged to set a standard.

Another means of testing would be to use standard free-hand movements, such as chins, push-ups, squat jumps, sit-ups, and the standing broad jump. This type of test should be used infrequently, however, to avoid having the practice of the test movements affect the results. Testing at the start, mid-point, and end of the weight training program should show results of strength gains primarily, whereas more frequent testing would strongly involve the factor of practice.

Certain performances will rate as outstanding. A man able to perform a single press with a barbell equal to his own body weight has developed superior strength. Fifty pounds in excess of body weight is unusual, and approximately 100 pounds over body weight puts a man in the same class for strength with the world champions. In the supine press, 50 pounds over body-weight indicates superior strength, while anyone should be able to exceed his own weight by a few pounds in this lift after three to five months of regular weight training. One hundred pounds over body weight is easily within the reach of an advanced weight trainer, and the strongest men exceed their own weight by 200 pounds in the press on bench.

In testing the arm flexors, a correct curl with 80 pounds under body weight is a respectable lift. Fifty to 30 pounds under body weight is a superior performance, while the strongest men are able to curl barbells closely approximating their own weight.

To test the legs, a full knee bend with a barbell equal to or a few pounds over body weight would be within the reach of any student. A man is developing superior strength when he can squat with 50 pounds over his own weight, and 100 pounds over body weight can be attained by regular hard training. The strongest men squat with 200 to 300 pounds more than their own weight.

The dead weight lift is a good test of basic strength, particularly of the back, legs, and grip. A lift of 150 pounds over body weight is within anyone's reach, and 200 pounds over body weight indicates superior strength. Advanced men can dead lift

300 pounds more than their weight, and the champions can straighten up with 400 to 500 pounds over body weight in this test.

It should be remembered that the weights in relation to the body weight discussed are approximations, referring primarily to men of average size. Smaller men will usually lift more, in proportion to their size, than larger men.

A sit-up with 25 pounds held behind the head (feet held down) shows reasonably good development of abdominal muscles,* and 50 to 75 pounds in this lift indicates superior strength in the mid-section. A few men have come within 50 pounds of their own weight in this lift.

A list of outstanding performances in exercise lifts follows. Official records in these lifts are not kept, so this is not an attempt to rate the best men, but only to indicate the possibilities of human strength. A list of outstanding press lifts, and performance on the other tests used in competition, appears at the end of the chapter on competitive lifting.

Supine press on bench

Doug Hepburn, weighing approximately 300 pounds, pressed a 560-pound barbell while lying supine. The weight was handed to him at straight arms, from where he lowered it to his chest and pushed it up to locked arms again. Hepburn also pressed 500 pounds on bench, with a two-second stop at the chest. Paul Anderson, weighing 330-340 pounds, was able to press 515 pounds in the supine position. Marvin Eder, weighing 195 pounds, supine pressed 480 pounds. Charles Vinci, weighing 125 pounds, supine pressed 325 pounds. In making these lifts, the men did not bridge up from the benches on which they were lying. (They did not arch and raise their buttocks to improve leverage.)

---

* Most of the work is done by the iliopsoas.

Curl with barbell

Jim Park, weighing 195 pounds, curled a 190-pound barbell. John Davis, weighing approximately 220 pounds, curled 205 pounds. Al Berger, heavyweight, reverse curled (curled with knuckles up) 175 pounds.

Full knee bend

Paul Anderson, weighing 330-340 pounds, made three repetition full squats with 900 pounds. Henry Steinborn, weighing approximately 210 pounds, squatted unassisted with 550 pounds (rocking the weight to his shoulders after raising one end). Tommy Kono, weighing 175 pounds, squatted with 450 pounds while holding the weight at his chest. Dave Moyer, weighing 123 pounds and less than 5 feet tall, squatted with 400 pounds.

Dead weight lift

Bob Peoples, weighing only 189 pounds, raised 725 pounds in the regular dead weight lift. This is more than the best dead lifts of Davis (705) and Rigoulot (621), both of whom cleaned and jerked 402 pounds. Peoples specialized on the dead lift, however, while Davis and Rigoulot did not. Little John Terry, 63 inches tall and weighing 135 to 140 pounds, made an amazing dead lift of 610 pounds. Terry had long arms and short legs, which gave him unusually favorable leverage in this lift. Herman Goerner, a full-fledged heavyweight, is reported to have made a dead lift with 793¾ pounds in 1920.

Sit-up with weight

Frank Leight, a New York City policeman who won the "Mr. America" title in 1942, performed one hundred repetition sit-ups with a 60-pound weight behind his head. Leight, who weighed 210 pounds at 71½ inches in height, made a single sit-up while holding 154 pounds behind his head. Dr. C. H. McCloy was able to do twenty sit-ups with 20 pounds behind his head on a 40-degree incline at the age of sixty-eight.

Chapter 8

Resistance Exercises for Football Players

THERE are probably many football coaches who insist that their players not use weight training, because to work against heavy resistance would make their charges "muscle-bound." These same coaches are probably the ones who work their boys hardest on the charging sled, with their heaviest line coach going along for the ride. No, they wouldn't want their men practicing resistance exercises!

Admittedly, experiments in the use of weight training have been made by football players, among other athletic specialists, in a haphazard and uncoordinated manner for the most part;

114

but the results obtained by a number of men who gained All-America recognition indicates that barbell-dumbbell exercise may have helped, and certainly did not hinder them. The greatest value of weight training for football players seems to be in cases where it is begun at the high school level, though it has also been used as a conditioner by college and professional players. Examples include: fullback Alan Ameche (Wisconsin, Baltimore Colts), tackle Stan Jones (Maryland, Chicago Bears), guard Alex Aronis (Navy), tackle-guard Walter Barnes (Louisiana State University, Philadelphia Eagles), and halfback Steve Van Buren (L.S.U., Eagles).

Ameche, Jones, and Aronis all began using the weights as high school boys, while Barnes first lifted as an already powerful collegian. From observation of successful weight-trained football players, it is quite possible that athletes in this sport could benefit from merely following an all-around course in basic exercise, as described in this book. Jones and Aronis did just that, and Aronis put such emphasis on body-building exercises that he gained fame in popular weight training magazines for having developed a flexed arm of 18 inches while still eighteen years of age. He was only 68 inches tall, however, and required great mobility and speed to be an effective running guard and linebacker while weighing under 190 pounds.

The taller Jones also became very powerful, and developed from 190 pounds (as a high school senior, after several months of weight training) to a playing weight of 250. He became so strong that the first time he tried to lift a pair of 100-pound dumbbells simultaneously, he succeeded easily in this difficult feat.

From the experience of successful players, and from a study of muscle development as applied to those muscles most used by football players (*See* Figure 34.), it is possible to set up a program which could be used by teams or individuals as preconditioning or between-seasons training:

1. Clean and press, light weight, ten repetitions.
2. Heavy press, ten repetitions.
3. Squat:
   Linemen, five repetitions, four sets.
   Backs, three repetitions, five sets.
4. Ten pullovers, light weight (emphasizing breathing).
5. Wrestler's bridge with weight, ten repetitions.

Optional

6. Sit-up with weight, fifteen repetitions.
7. Curl, ten repetitions.
8. Rowing exercise, ten repetitions.
9. Supine press, ten repetitions.
10. Running, other pre-equipment training.

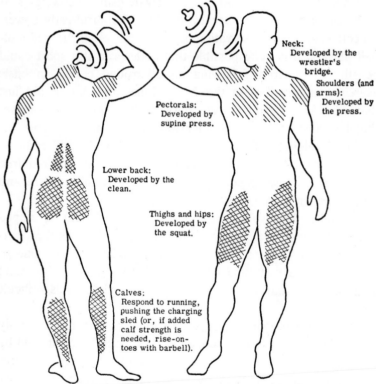

Figure 34. Muscles especially valuable in football.

This program would be just about impossible to continue throughout the season, once equipment is issued and scrimmage begun, unless some of the exercises were practiced in the locker room or gym before donning pads. Once work on the charging sled and vigorous blocking is begun, there is little need for additional leg exercise. The exercises most valuable in this case are overhead pressing to limber shoulders stiffened by blocking and tackling, and the wrestler's bridge to maintain neck strength and help avoid injury.

The full program is primarily intended as a preconditioning routine for the first week or two of practice, or for use by individual players during the summer months. If used individually during the off season, one or two days per week of alternate jogging and sprinting (for at least a half mile) is recommended. The program could be set up with weight training Mondays, Wednesdays, and Fridays; running Tuesdays and Thursdays.

If used as part of formal team training, it would still be wise to work with the weights as special exercises on alternate days, using other conditioning drills on the off days. For example:

Monday—Weight training and football fundamentals.
Tuesday—Sprints, simple tumbling, and football fundamentals.
Wednesday and Friday—Same as Monday.
Thursday—Same as Tuesday.

At this point it is appropriate to digress and describe a special remedial exercise that has been used successfully in many cases to strengthen injured knees, one of the most common injuries to football players. The exercise is performed by attaching weight to the foot of the injured leg. The athlete sits on a sturdy table with his thigh supported to the knee, the weighted foot hanging free. He then extends the foot until the leg is straight, contracting the muscles of the thigh and concentrating on those around the knee. (*See* Figure 35.)

This exercise is specially valuable for two reasons: (1) It is non-weight bearing (The body's weight is taken off the injured joint.), thus allowing the lightest possible start in working back to normal strength. (2) It puts the work exactly where it is needed to overcome the weakness. Weighted sandals, which are designed to take additional weight, and which can be strapped to the feet, are available commercially. The extension exercise will bring good results if practiced in four or five sets of five to ten repetitions, with brief rests (about three minutes) after each set. The weight should be increased by 2½ to 5 pounds whenever the repetitions are completed easily. If the athlete is able to continue regular practice, the extension exercise should be performed first. The leg extension, working both legs, is a good preventative measure if practiced before a knee injury has been incurred.

Figure 35. Remedial exercise for injured knee.

The leg extension exercise with weights was used at Texas Christian University, where trainer Elmer Brown was quoted as saying, "Those weight lifting exercises with the foot are the best thing I've seen for a post-operative knee or one which is just naturally weak." Among the T.C.U. players on whom the resistance exercises proved helpful was All-America linebacker Keith Flowers.

There is some question about the effect of full squats on the knees. It is possible that going into the full knee bend position may place unnecessary strain on the joints, since it is possible to develop great strength in the legs while working over a more limited range. Modern football players do not start from a deeply flexed leg position. In fact, their legs are bent little past the right angle position and are even further extended before the resistance of meeting an opponent is met.

For this reason, coaches may prefer to have their charges practice squats to the point where the thighs are only parallel to the floor. A simple method of doing this is to have the athletes squat to a box 12 to 14 inches high. This will take taller men past parallel, but well above the full bend that may adversely affect the knee joint. It is quite possible that full bends will not injure a normal knee, so if individual athletes prefer to squat all the way down there is no reason why they should not try it. Many outstanding football players and other athletes have practiced full squats with heavy weights without any apparent adverse effect.

Unquestionably, squatting movements are the key exercise between seasons for football players, especially linemen. Not only do they develop strong thighs, but they tend to increase the body weight of husky young men who naturally gravitate toward football. Developing the strength to squat with a barbell heavier than the heaviest opponent also gives a player a psychological boost, since he can feel confident of blocking a bigger man effectively providing he carries out his assignment properly.

The other general strengthening exercises are also important, especially those which work the shoulders and neck, for developing muscular shock-absorbing pads as well as strength.

If a coach were unable to obtain sufficient barbell equipment to work a large group on a complete exercise routine, but still had one or two barbells available, one or two exercises practiced at the players' initiative would still provide valuable extra strength. In this case, the players could be instructed to train on repetition overhead presses and repetition squats. Each man should do five-ten presses and fifteen squats with a weight that will extend him to work hard on the last three or four repetitions. If only these two exercises are to be done, and if time permits, the exercises should be repeated in sets. One way to do this is to do ten presses with a given weight, then rest briefly and do seven-eight more presses with an additional 10 pounds, followed by another rest period and four-five more presses with a final 10-pound increase. The squats should be done the same way, but with more weight and with twelve, eight, and five repetitions. Another method of using just two exercises is to take a given weight for the press, and a heavier poundage for the squat, and do each exercise ten repetitions, three times (three sets).

To increase the throwing distance of forward passers with accuracy but little strength, a special exercise is suggested by Dr. C. H. McCloy, of the State University of Iowa. The exercise is performed lying supine with a barbell held at locked arms directly over the chest. The athlete keeps his arms straight and simply shrugs his shoulders forward and upward as far as possible five to ten repetitions. This movement should be repeated in three or four sets, and it will be necessary to have assistants hand the weight to the exerciser and take it away, since it should be a heavier poundage than he can press into position himself.

While it might seem that it would be necessary only to use the exercises that strengthen specific muscles for sports in which they are used to a great extent, it is important that all-around strength be developed, as well as muscular shock-absorbers, as mentioned previously. D. G. Johnson and Oscar Heidenstam, English authors, have written: "We agree that it is necessary to strengthen the muscle groups required for performing a particular event, but at the same time if opposite groups and other muscles are completely neglected, it means not only one-sided development, but a distinct weakness in one of the antagonistic groups . . . We think that certain basic exercises are necessary for all events where there is a specific weakness in the muscle groups used . . . We do not expect the competitor to be a weight training specialist, but a good all-round basic schedule . . . will work wonders for every type of athlete."

It can be seen that while the legs are the propellant that puts drive into a good block, tackle, and buck into the line, arm and shoulder strength, as well as all-around body power, is important to defensive play in which any form of hand-fighting an opponent is used.

Chapter 9

Resistance Exercises for Basketball Players

IN describing weight training for basketball, we are fortunate in having a basic program which has been tried and proven effective around which to build an exercise routine. A program almost identical to the one to be listed was used by the varsity basketball squad of the State University of Iowa. At Iowa the program was worked out by Dr. C. H. McCloy, Dr. Arthur Wendler, Dr. Frank Sills, and graduate student Dick Garth, who was preparing a thesis on "The Effect of Weight Training on the Jumping Ability of Basketball Players." Garth found that the average jumping ability of the Hawkeye players improved 2.7 inches as measured by a standard jump-for-height test. In addition to improved jumping, Dr. McCloy reported that the players improved from 15 to 25 per cent in strength, and Coach Frank (Bucky) O'Connor said the weight training made his team "stronger physically for the rugged work under the baskets."

The first Iowa team to use the planned weight training as a group was predominantly composed of sophomores, but placed second in the Big Ten. As juniors, still using the weights, they won the conference championship.

A recommended weight training routine for basketball players is as follows:

1. Clean and press, ten repetitions, two sets.
2. Curl, ten repetitions, two sets.
3. Lateral raise, dumbbells, ten repetitions.
4. Forward raise, dumbbells, ten repetitions.
5. Squat, ten repetitions, two sets.
6. Pullover, ten repetitions with light weight after each set of squats.
7. Quick partial bends with barbell on shoulders, dipping to approximately one-quarter squat or as though to jump at center or try for a rebound.
8. Jumping to touch as high as possible on a basketball backboard marked off in inches from the floor; ten jumps to touch with the right hand and ten with the left. Highest jump progress with each hand should be noted.

The weight training routine used at Iowa was almost identical to the one listed above. At Iowa a variation of the squat was used in which the exerciser stood with one foot advanced about 12 to 16 inches in front of the other, then squatted until the heel of the rear foot touched the buttock on that side. The exerciser then rose, stepped forward to the 12-16 inch distance with the other foot, and squatted again, and so on for the desired number of counts. This type of squat was done to protect the knees from strain, since several had been weakened by previous injury.

Partial knee bends were not included in the routine used at

Iowa. In all the exercises except squats, the Iowans worked up from seven to ten repetitions and then added weight; in the "walking squat," they worked up from sixteen to twenty-four repetitions.

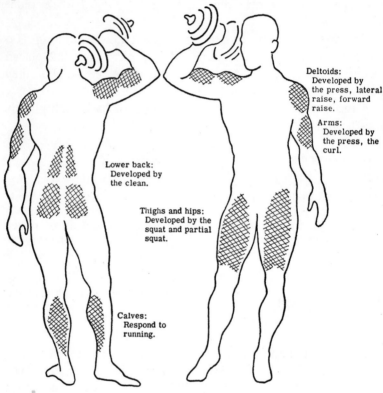

Deltoids:
Developed by the press, lateral raise, forward raise.

Arms:
Developed by the press, the curl.

Lower back:
Developed by the clean.

Thighs and hips:
Developed by the squat and partial squat.

Calves:
Respond to running.

Note: Pullover expands chest capacity.

Figure 36. Muscles especially valuable in basketball.

In addition to the weight training, the Iowa team was undergoing other conditioning exercises which had been a regular part of their practice sessions, and of course they were working on basketball fundamentals and plays. Other conditioning exercises used by Coach O'Connor were sit-ups (fifty repetitions), rope jumping, and running up and down the steps of the Iowa field-house. The weight training exercises were done three days weekly at Iowa, and this system is recommended. For example:

Monday—Weight training followed by regular practice.
Tuesday—Conditioning exercises and practice.
Wednesday—Same as Monday.
Thursday—Same as Tuesday.
Friday—Same as Monday and Wednesday.

A weight training routine can be ideal to develop strength in players who are "overgrown" to desirable height for basketball, but who lack sufficient muscle to move their frames with agility. (*See* Figure 36.) An example of success in overcoming awkwardness in a giant who became an effective varsity player was seen in Bill Simonovich, of the University of Minnesota. Simonovich was given a program of weight training and calisthenics by Coach Ozzie Cowles and became a capable rebounder and point-maker despite (or because of!) his 6 feet, 11 inches height, and 290 pounds weight.

A tall man needing to gain weight and strength could also be given the supine press on bench and the rowing motion for a time, simply to develop the large muscles of the chest and back to some extent for adding body weight. Once reasonably normal development is acquired, however, there is no point in continuing hypertrophy of these muscles, which add little to a basketball player's game performance.

The leg-extension movement with weight on the feet (described for football players) can be used to rehabilitate knees injured in basketball.

Chapter 10

Resistance Exercises for Baseball Players

WEIGHT training for baseball players must emphasize development of the muscles that aid in running, throwing, and batting, as well as provide general strength and muscle tone. (*See* Figure 37.) Many big league ball players have used weight training to various extents, most notable among them being pitcher Bob Feller and batting champion Ralph Kiner.

A barbell and dumbbell routine recommended for baseball players follows:

1. Clean and press, ten repetitions, light weight.
2. Alternate press with dumbbells (pressing one weight up while

lowering the other, using a rocking, see-saw motion), ten repetitions each arm, two sets (pressing with speed).

3. Squat, five repetitions, four sets.
4. Light pullover, ten repetitions after each set of squats.
5. Sit-up with weight behind head, twisting to touch elbows to opposite knees, alternately.
6. Supine press, ten repetitions.
7. Straight arm lateral raise, ten repetitions.
8. Throwing motion using pulley weight, twenty to thirty "throws."

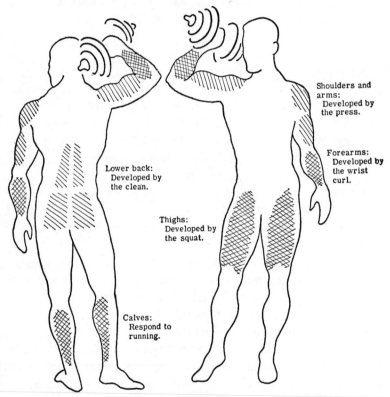

Figure 37. Muscles especially valuable in baseball.

The throwing motion is not necessary if outdoor practice has begun, but is helpful for ballplayers working out indoors during cold or rainy weather.

Because all baseball players do a lot of throwing, the forward shrugging of the shoulders while holding a barbell at straight arms over the chest in the supine position is a good exercise. Dr. C. H. McCloy, of Iowa, says this exercise (described in the chapter on exercise for football) has been shown to have favorable effect on all throwing athletes. The arms should remain straight, supporting the weight, while the shoulders are alternately brought forward and then lowered over as much range of movement as possible. The exercise should add speed to a pitch, and distance to an outfielder's peg to hold base runners to minimum advance.

Strong wrists and forearms are important to ballplayers, especially in batting. By sitting with the forearms supported on the thighs to the wrists, and with a barbell in the hands, it is possible to perform a wrist curling motion that works the forearm muscles strongly. With palms up, the weight is lowered so that it hangs at the end of the fingers and then raised by closing the hand and bending the wrist upward as far as possible. The same action can be done with palms down, but the grip of the thumb will prevent the weight being lowered as far as when it is allowed to roll down in the fingers. This wrist curl should be done two or three sets of ten repetitions.

Another exercise for the forearms is done by loading a dumbbell at one end and holding the unloaded end in the hand, with the arm straight down at the side. Then the weighted end of the dumbbell is raised as far forward as possible by bending the wrist, keeping the arm stationary at the side. The same exercise can be done with the weight extending to the back, raising it as far as possible backward. If this exercise is done with the wrist curl, one set of ten repetitions should be done in each direction.

Squeezing a rubber ball, or a spring tension gripper, is another means of developing strong forearms.

The baseball program is good for year-'round conditioning, but would bring good results if done only during the one or two months immediately preceding the start of the season. Few ballplayers will have the time or ambition to continue the weight training schedule once the season is underway, but practice of squats and rapid alternate presses will serve to loosen the muscles and keep up strength if practiced occasionally.

The weight training program described for baseball players should be used three days per week; Mondays, Wednesdays, and Fridays are recommended. It is suggested that some "speed game," such as handball or basketball, be practiced on two or three of the alternate days, as an aid in conditioning and hand-and-eye coordination.

An example of a star baseball player (and also an All-America calibre football player at the University of California) who derived benefit from weight training is Jackie Jensen, outfielder for the Boston Red Sox. Jensen took to barbell training while a schoolboy in an attempt to overcome a shoulder injury incurred while throwing a baseball. Jensen quotes his doctor as saying he would "never be able to throw hard again." In Jensen's words, "I went to the YMCA gym in Oakland and began doing some weight lifting. I was a really skinny kid at the time, but this weight lifting built up my body. . . ."

Jensen continued exercising, served a hitch in the navy, and then played football and baseball in college. He said, "The arm was as good as new and it's stayed that way."

Chapter 11

Resistance Exercises for Track and Field

IT is in track and field that much experimentation with weight training has been done by top-ranking competitors. Men like Bob Richards, Mal Whitfield, Otis Chandler, Parry O'Brien, Fortune Gordien, and Bob Backus have shown that weight training can be a positive asset to runners, jumpers, and throwers alike.

Having won top honors in pole vaulting at the Olympics, and United States championships in the Decathlon and All-Around, Bob Richards is an outstanding example showing that a man can lift weights and be an enduring, fast-moving, and superbly-coordinated athlete. He began practicing standard weight lifting exercises while twelve years of age and was outstanding at basketball and football before specializing in track and field.

Richards practiced little weight training exercise for his legs, fearing that to do so would result in increased muscle size, the weight of which would handicap his vaulting. He did work his legs with an extension movement, using weights attached to his feet, especially on one occasion when he was hospitalized for an appendectomy prior to the 1948 Olympiad. He credits this exercise, plus the pressing of a barbell while lying supine in his hospital bed, with enabling him to resume hard training after his convalescence with the result that he made the U.S. Olympic team. In his regular training program, Richards prepared for the pole vault as follows:

1. Approximately thirty vaults.
2. Five to ten 60-yard wind sprints.
3. Rope climbing.
4. Fifteen to twenty minutes of weight training.
5. Freehand exercises and gymnastics, such as chinning, and press-ups into the handstand position.

The specific weight training movements Richards used were the clean and press, the curl, the reverse curl, the pullover, and leg-raises with five-pound weights attached to each foot. Richards practiced pressing in decreasing repetitions, starting with five with 135 pounds, and cutting the repetitions gradually as he worked up in weight to a single press with 160 pounds. His curls were done with about 70 pounds for six to ten repetitions. These exercises developed strength for pulling up on the pole and pushing off to clear the cross-bar. The leg-raising movement, which Richards did ten to twenty repetitions, is one which contributes to both abdominal and thigh strength.

Incidentally, Richards occasionally added variety to his weight training program by practicing the lifts used in competition. On one occasion, he made a dozen single cleans and jerks with 225 pounds. This lift requires, and conversely develops, all-around coordinated strength and great explosive power. Richards' lifts, made at a weight of approximately 160 pounds, would have rated him a worthy contender for middleweight honors in smaller AAU district weight lifting contests. Richards' best performances in track and field events, at the time he was practicing the above weight training exercises, were as follows: 100-meter dash, 10.9 seconds; broad jump, 23 feet; 16-pound shot put, 43 feet; high jump, 6 feet-1 inch; 400-meter run, 51.6 seconds; 110-meter high hurdles, 15.2 seconds; javelin throw, 196 feet; pole vault, 15 feet-4¾ inches; 1500-meter run, 4:51.0; discus throw, 136 feet.

Mal Whitfield's approach to weight training seems at first surprising, but is logical upon investigation. In view of his great ability at various distances, it is worth careful consideration. Whitfield, two-time Olympic Games 800-meter running champion, felt that his practice on the track provided him with all the endurance he needed, so his weight training was designed to produce maximum strength by using heavy weights and low repetitions.

Whitfield did his barbell/dumbbell exercises in sets of five or three repetitions, using incredible poundages for a 73 inches tall middle distance runner weighing 170 pounds. He practiced full squats in five sets of three repetitions, a total of fifteen squats, with the barbell loaded to 255-270 pounds. Other exercises included bent-arm pullovers (again using heavy weights, to 250 pounds), straight-arm pullovers, overhead presses, supine presses, and sit-up with feet elevated on an incline while holding 25 pounds behind his head. Two exercises that were special favorites were the one-legged squat (alternating legs for five repetitions) while holding 50-75 pounds, and an arm swinging movement, similar to the action of running (practiced in running stance) while holding 10- to 25-pound dumbbells in each hand.

It should be emphasized, however, that Whitfield did not continue this strenuous weight training through the track season, but discontinued it when he began running competitively. With him, weight training was an out-of-season conditioner.

For runners and jumpers the following exercises are recommended:

RUNNERS AND HURDLERS

1. Clean and press, ten repetitions.
2. Squat, three repetitions, five sets.
3. Pullover, ten repetitions with light weight after each set of squats.
4. Curl, ten repetitions.
5. Supine press, ten repetitions.

JUMPERS

Same as runners' program, but with the addition of *quick* partial bends with heavier weights on shoulders, ten repetitions, three sets. The knee dip should be to no more than one-quarter squat position, flat-footed, and with body erect. This exercise should be practiced after the full knee bend.

POLE VAULTERS

1. Clean and press, light weight, ten repetitions.
2. Heavy press, three repetitions, four sets.
3. Curl, eight repetitions, two sets.
4. Reverse curl (knuckles up), eight repetitions, two sets.
5. Partial knee bends (see jumpers' program).
6. Pullover, ten repetitions after each set of partial squats.
7. Leg-raise, fifteen-twenty repetitions, preferably with a 5-pound weight on each foot.

The programs advocated for track, and field events not classed as weight throwing, are prescribed for use as out-of-season training. (*See* Figure 38.) Of course the runners and jumpers will want to continue some form of work on the track or roadwork in the off season as well. Vaulters should include some gymnastics, rope climbing, and similar exercises. The weight training movements should be done only three days per week, especially if the athlete is training at all strenuously on an indoor or outdoor track. Note the partial bend exercise recommended for jumpers and vaulters. This exercise will develop strength and spring over approximately the same range of action used in a take-off, and has the added advantage of being one which will produce strength without having much effect on muscle size. With Bob Richards' concern about body weight in mind, this is the only leg exercise listed for vaulters. Vaulters

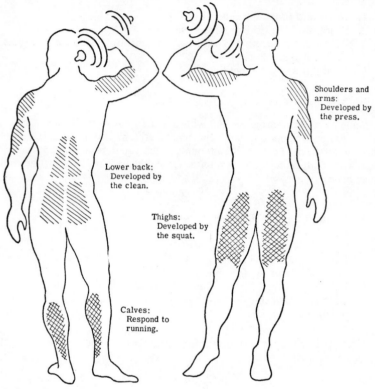

Note: Pullover expands chest capacity.

Figure 38. Muscles especially valuable in track events.

seeking additional leg strength, however, may experiment with the jumpers' leg program, meanwhile keeping a check on body weight. It is probable that athletes following a rigorous program, which includes considerable running, will not add weight appreciably to their legs even if they practice full squats.

Otis Chandler, one of the first men to put the 16-pound shot more than 57 feet, was an enthusiastic weight trainer (and competitive lifter) who made a study of the use of weights by track and field men. He learned that seven of the first eleven shot putters to pass 56 feet used weight training exercises, and was unable to obtain data on two. Chandler was of the opinion that the two who said they did not use weight training, Charles Fonville and Jim Fuchs, would have been better shot putters if they had. Chandler recommended exercises like those listed for weight men and advocated standing leg-raises with weights on the feet for jumpers and runners.

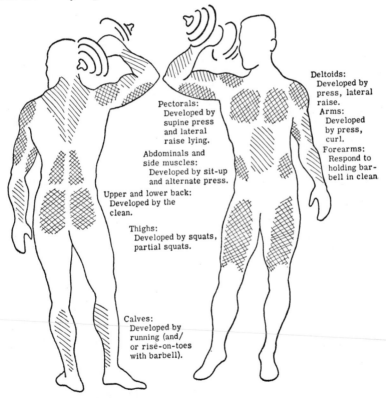

Pectorals:
Developed by
supine press
and lateral
raise lying.

Abdominals and
side muscles:
Developed by sit-up
and alternate press.

Upper and lower back:
Developed by the
clean.

Thighs:
Developed by squats,
partial squats.

Deltoids:
Developed by
press, lateral
raise.

Arms:
Developed
by press,
curl.

Forearms:
Respond to
holding bar-
bell in clean.

Calves:
Developed by
running (and/
or rise-on-toes
with barbell).

Figure 39. Muscles especially valuable in field events.

For shot putters, discus throwers, hammer throwers, and javelin throwers, it is suggested that at least one or two months be devoted to the twelve basic exercises in the chapter on fundamental weight training. Men competing in the throwing events need all-around strength and will find that such strength will benefit them in whatever event they enter. (*See* Figure 39.) Suggested pre-season (one or two months before and up to the beginning of actual practice of the event) training is as follows:

SHOT PUT

1. Clean and press, ten repetitions, light weight.
2. Alternate press, heavy dumbbells; five repetitions with each hand, four sets.
3. Squat, five repetitions, four sets.
4. Pullover, ten repetitions.
5. Sit-up with weight behind head, twisting to touch elbows to opposite knees alternately, twenty repetitions.
6. Supine press, five repetitions, four sets.
   For the shot putter the head end of the bench should be raised so that the angle at which the barbell is pressed is approximately the angle at which the shot is released.

DISCUS THROW

The same program will serve for the discus thrower, with the addition of a lateral raise exercise, lying, three sets of ten repetitions. Fortune Gordien also used the lateral raise, standing, for added deltoid strength, the rise-on-toes for calf spring, and a "dumbbell discus throw" movement. He would wind up for the throw and go through the acceleration of turning to bring the weight up to shoulder level. Immediately after following a weight training program (which he continued during early throwing practice days), Gordien set a world record of 194 feet, 6 inches.

HAMMER THROW

For the hammer thrower, the shot putters' routine will again prove basically sound, but additional work should be included to develop strength over short-range leg extension and in the trapezius. Three sets of at least three (attempting to do five) cleans are invaluable power builders. This is not the competitive style clean of the weight lifter, but an all-the-way-up pull from floor to shoulders without moving the feet, and with only slight knee dip to receive the weight at the chest. The cleans should be started with the erect crouch described previously. The upright rowing exercise, working up from eight to twelve repetitions and adding weight, is another good movement for the hammer thrower.

Bob Backus, who set records in the 35- and 56-pound weight throws, emphasized heavy squats, cleans, and supine presses in his weight training program. He also did two sets of shoulder shrugging movements, using 380 pounds for ten repetitions, and heavy partial squats (approximately one-quarter knee dip) with 600 pounds on his shoulders for three sets of ten repetitions.

JAVELIN THROW

1. Clean and press, ten repetitions, light weight.
2. Alternate press, dumbbells; ten repetitions each arm, two sets (pressing with speed).
3. Squat, five repetitions, four sets.
4. Pullover, ten repetitions after each set of squats (using light weight).
5. Sit-up with weight behind head, twisting to touch elbows to opposite knees, alternately. If possible the javelin thrower should do sit-ups with his legs supported only to the buttocks, so his torso can back-bend slightly at the low point.
6. Supine press, five repetitions, four sets.
7. Straight-arm lateral raise, ten repetitions.
8. Throwing motion using pulley weight, ten to twenty "throws." A section of javelin handle, with grip binding, can be attached to the pulley rope, or the regular pulley handle can be held in the hand.
9. Chinning or rope climbing.

The exercise suggested by Dr. McCloy, shrugging forward while lying supine with a barbell at straight arms over the chest, should be used by shot, discus, and javelin men whenever possible. McCloy says that exercise develops the serratus anterior muscle, which is important in throwing due to its function of pulling the scapula forward. Because the action is over a very short range, the exercise can easily be practiced three sets of ten repetitions without fatigue, even though heavy weights are used. McCloy believes this exercise can increase distance in the discus throw by as much at 15 feet.

It is difficult to say which of the weight training movements are most valuable for participants in the sports covered in this chapter, but the exercises that appear in every schedule are the clean, press, and squat. It is possible to develop the abdominal muscles by sit-ups and leg-raises without weight (though more strength is acquired through using resistance) and the arms and upper back by chinning. The triceps and pectorals will respond · to dipping (on parallel bars and in the "push-up") but not to the extent that they will with more than the body's weight. For complete development of shoulder and arm strength, however, there is no better exercise than the overhead press with barbell or dumbbells. No exercise is better than the squat with barbell on shoulders to develop sheer strength in the legs. No other form of exercise remotely approaches lifting a barbell from the floor for development of the powerful muscles of the lower back. For these reasons, the clean, press, and squat with barbell should be practiced to some degree by every athlete who wants to give his best possible performance.

Chapter 12

Weight Training for the "Minor" Sports

WHILE, of course, there are no "minor" sports, insofar as benefit to participants is concerned, we make the distinction on a basis of spectator interest in the United States. There is no sport, which is truly an athletic event, in which increased strength will not benefit a participant to some extent.

Resistance exercises for wrestlers

There is probably no sport in which strength can be applied with greater effectiveness than wrestling (*See* Figure 40.) An

139

example of a weight-trained grappler is Henry Wittenberg, eight times U.S. National AAU champion and winner of the 191-pound class at the 1948 Olympic games. Wittenberg, of course, practiced intensively on the mat and also ran for endurance, but

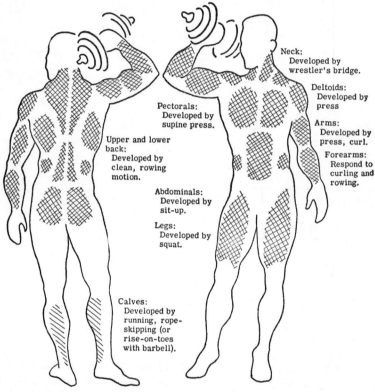

Neck:
Developed by
wrestler's bridge.

Deltoids:
Developed by
press

Pectorals:
Developed by
supine press.

Arms:
Developed by
press, curl.

Upper and lower
back:
Developed by
clean, rowing
motion.

Forearms:
Respond to
curling and
rowing.

Abdominals:
Developed by
sit-up.

Legs:
Developed by
squat.

Calves:
Developed by
running, rope-
skipping (or
rise-on-toes
with barbell).

Note: Pullover expands chest capacity.
Oblique muscles at sides of abdomen can receive additional strengthening by
alternate press with dumbbells or side-bends with weight held in one hand.

Figure 40. Muscles especially valuable in wrestling.

the simplified weight training routine he followed throughout his fifteen years of competition might well be adopted by any wrestler. Wittenberg practiced three barbell exercises regularly: Overhead pressing, rowing pulls to the body while leaning forward, and squatting with barbell on shoulders. He regularly used 180 pounds for three sets of ten repetitions in each exercise, but astounded members of the Olympic weight lifting team, on the occasion of his first workout with them, when he pressed 198 pounds ten repetitions. Wittenberg also worked with dumbbells in a variety of exercises, using as much as 60 pounds in each hand.

The use of heavy weights for fairly high repetitions would seem ideally suited to the wrestler, especially if he can approximate the weight of an opponent on the barbell in some of the exercises. The following program is recommended:

1. Clean and press, light weight, ten repetitions.
2. Heavy press, ten repetitions, three sets.
3. Squat, ten (or fifteen) repetitions, three sets.
4. Ten straight-arm pullovers with a light weight after each set of squats.
5. Rowing exercise, ten repetitions, three sets.

Optional

6. Wrestler's bridge with weight on chest, ten repetitions.
7. Sit-up with weight, fifteen repetitions.
8. Curl, ten repetitions, two sets.
9. Supine press, ten repetitions, two sets.
10. Rope skipping or running, and practice on mat.

Resistance exercises for swimmers

Swimming champion Dick Cleveland (Ohio State University) is another interesting example of a weight-trained athletic specialist, exploding the unfounded taboo that "swimming muscles" and "lifting muscles" are different. (*See* Figure 41.) Cleveland practiced weight training under the supervision of Fraysher Ferguson at his gymnasium in Columbus, Ohio. The swimmer exercised with weights five days per week, with the following program:

Mondays, Wednesdays, and Fridays:

Warm-up with bending and stretching calisthenics.
Supine press on bench, barbell.
Press on inclined bench.
Dumbbell flying motions (lateral raise) supine on bench.
Overhead pressing, standing and seated, barbell.
Alternate press with dumbbells. (All exercises done eight-twelve repe-
    titions in three sets with full, deep, oral breathing.)

Tuesdays and Thursdays:

Warm-up with calisthenics.
Four to five sets of ten repetition full, bouncing squats.
Deep breathing pullovers with light weight after each set of squats.

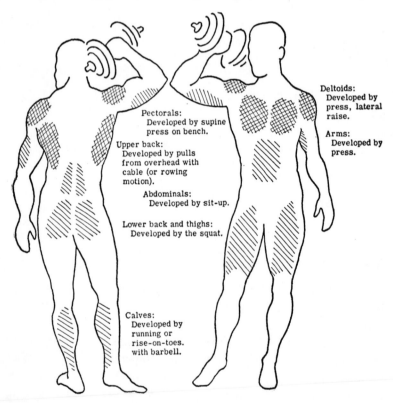

Deltoids:
   Developed by
   press, lateral
   raise.

Arms:
   Developed by
   press.

Pectorals:
   Developed by supine
   press on bench.

Upper back:
   Developed by pulls
   from overhead with
   cable (or rowing
   motion).

Abdominals:
   Developed by sit-up.

Lower back and thighs:
   Developed by the squat.

Calves:
   Developed by
   running or
   rise-on-toes.
   with barbell.

Figure 41. Muscles especially valuable in swimming.

After six weeks with this program, Cleveland was able to perform three sets of ten wide-grip supine presses with 170 pounds and three sets of ten full squats with 200 pounds on his shoulders. He weighed 160 pounds, in excellent athletic condition, at the start of the program and weighed 178 pounds at the end of six weeks. The best testimony to the results of the program is the fact that Cleveland established a world outdoor 50-meter freestyle swimming record just two weeks later! He had not practiced swimming during the six-week period of weight training.

Among other Ohio State swimmers who achieved good results under Ferguson's tutelage was Al Wiggins, who set records in the butterfly and medley (freestyle, backstroke, and butterfly) races. Wiggins' program is one that could be used for Monday-Wednesday-Friday training by any swimmer:

1. Sit-up on inclined board.
2. Press.
3. Pull-ups (upright rowing with leg and back start).
4. Press on bench.
5. Alternate dumbbell press.
6. Squat.
7. Curl.
8. Lateral raise.
9. Pulls from overhead to waist and to back of neck, using bar with cable through pulley to suspended weights.

Wiggins, who increased his weight from 180 to 206 pounds at a height of 76 inches, broke the record for the 150 yard medley race by more than five seconds with 1:24.4. He developed great strength, making a single press on bench with over 300 pounds. It is easy to see how muscles strengthened by weight training could help propel a swimmer through the water by increased stroking and kicking power.

The exercises are not limited to use by men, for a weight training program was employed with good results by the Town Club of Chicago girls' swimming team in 1952. The girls exercised with weights Mondays, Wednesdays, and Fridays, including the following exercises: Lateral raises, one-arm presses, one-arm curls, regular curls, presses, presses behind neck, squats, dead lifts, supine lateral raises, reverse curls, Jefferson lifts, pullovers, and supine presses. This complete weight training routine was followed for one hour prior to swimming practice. Results noted by Coach Walter Schlueter were that the girls improved in stamina, power, speed, general health, and posture. The Town Club relay team set a world record for 400 yards at the national championships that year. Many of the club members were participants in the 1952 Olympics.

Resistance exercises for boxers

For the most part, successful boxers are of the physical type that would be classified as predominantly mesomorphic. These men appear muscular and are strong as a result of their general training, so it might seem that weight training is superfluous. A number of weight-trained men have become successful boxers, however, so it is possible that the strength they developed from lifting weights may have helped them in their pugilistic careers. (*See* Figure 42.) Among the more successful boxers who used weights before or during their competitive days were Olympic champion Bill Bossio and professionals Randy Turpin and Bob Baker.

The primary concern of the following program is to develop strength in the arms and shoulders for punching power, but exercises are included to strengthen the legs, and develop the neck and abdominal muscles to act as shock absorbers:

1. Alternate press with dumbbells, driving arms up to full lock rapidly.
2. Alternate curl from sides to shoulders with dumbbells.
3. Supine press with barbell, hands spaced slightly wider than the points of the shoulders.
4. Full squats or squats to knee-height bench with barbell across shoulders.
5. Bent-arm lateral raise lying supine on bench.

6. Sit-up with weight behind head, preferably with feet at high end of board slanted 10 to 20 degrees.
7. Wrestler's bridge with weight held on chest.
8. Running or rope-skipping, and punching light and heavy bags.

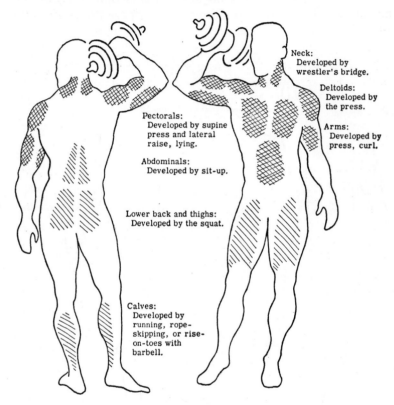

Figure 42. Muscles especially valuable in boxing.

The weight resistance exercises should be done two or three sets of ten repetitions (for *each* arm in the movements with alternate action). It might seem that the pressing would be far more important than curling, due to its similarity to punching, but it is also important to develop the biceps in order to maintain strongly bent arms when hooking.

Resistance exercises for oarsmen

Weight training was a part of the training regimen of Jack Kelly, Jr. (winner of many single sculls championships) during his four-months winter layoff from rowing. (*See* Figure 43.) He

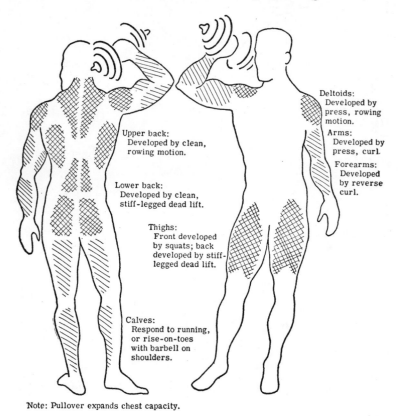

Deltoids:
Developed by
press, rowing
motion.

Arms:
Developed by
press, curl.

Forearms:
Developed
by reverse
curl.

Upper back:
Developed by clean,
rowing motion.

Lower back:
Developed by clean,
stiff-legged dead lift.

Thighs:
Front developed
by squats; back
developed by stiff-
legged dead lift.

Calves:
Respond to running,
or rise-on-toes
with barbell on
shoulders.

Note: Pullover expands chest capacity.

Figure 43. Muscles especially valuable in rowing.

practiced several exercises ten repetitions, adding weight whenever he could exceed ten. He pulled weights of from 120 to 150 pounds to his chest in the rowing motion, and pressed 100 to 120 pounds overhead. At the same time, his training included regular push-ups, chins, and squat jumps, as well as work on the rowing machine and running. Kelly, who began using weights at the age of fourteen, said, "I found that weight training would aid my strength, but I stick to running and long steady rowing to build up my endurance. . . ."

A recommended program for oarsmen is as follows:

1. Clean and press, ten repetitions.
2. Rapid alternate press with dumbbells, ten repetitions each arm.
3. Squat, moving rapidly, three sets of ten repetitions. (These squats can be finished with a jump into the air if a light weight is used.)
4. Pullover, ten repetitions after each set of squats.
5. Sit-up with weight behind head, fifteen repetitions, three sets.
6. Curl, ten repetitions.
7. Reverse curl, ten repetitions.
8. Rowing exercise, three sets of ten repetitions.
9. Stiff-legged dead lift, three sets of ten repetitions.

Resistance exercises for tennis players

With weight training used in the programs of such Australian tennis champions as Frank Sedgman, it seems evident that added strength will aid in getting the ball across the net with more speed. Strong wrists, in addition, will help place the ball, by improving the ease with which players handle the racquet.

1. Clean and press, ten repetitions.
2. Rapid alternate press with dumbbells, ten repetitions, each arm.
3. Curl, ten repetitions.
4. Reverse curl, ten repetitions.
5. Rapid squat, ten repetitions, two sets.
6. Pullover, ten repetitions after each set of squats.
7. Bent-arm lateral raise, supine.
8. Forearm exercises. (See description under training program for baseball players.)

Resistance exercises for golfers

The success of golf champion Frank Stranahan indicates that A-1 play on the links can be combined with medal-winning weight lifting. Stranahan handled such commendable poundages as 300 clean and jerk, 400 squat, and more than 500 dead lift, training with the heaviest weights he could lift during the same years he was doing his best golfing. Stranahan believed the lifting helped his golf, but said if he had to give up one sport or the other, he would give up golf! The weight training recommended for golfers is the same as that prescribed for tennis players (above), with the exception that golfers need not strive for speed in doing the squats. (*See* Figure 44.)

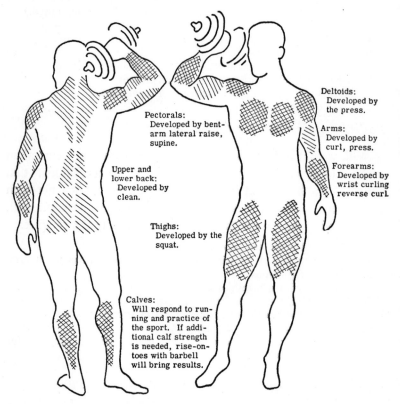

Pectorals:
Developed by bent-arm lateral raise, supine.

Upper and lower back:
Developed by clean.

Thighs:
Developed by the squat.

Calves:
Will respond to running and practice of the sport. If additional calf strength is needed, rise-on-toes with barbell will bring results.

Deltoids:
Developed by the press.

Arms:
Developed by curl, press.

Forearms:
Developed by wrist curling reverse curl.

Figure 44. Muscles especially valuable in tennis and golf.

Resistance exercises for fencers

The fencer should have strong legs, shoulders, and forearms in particular (*See* Figure 45.), so a weight training routine can be prescribed as follows:

1. Clean and press, ten repetitions, two sets.
2. Squat, ten repetitions, two sets.
3. Lunge to thrusting position with light barbell across shoulders, alternating legs; two sets of ten repetitions for each leg.
4. Ten pullovers with light weight, breathing deeply, after each set of squats and lunges.
5. Supine press on bench, ten repetitions.
6. Bent-arm lateral raise, supine, ten repetitions.
7. Alternate forward raise, dumbbells, ten repetitions, each arm.
8. Lateral raise standing, ten repetitions.
9. Forearm exercises. (Description in section for baseball players.)

We have seen that the weight training exercises practiced by successful specialist athletes have been remarkably similar, although with variations in the amount of weight handled and the number of repetitions and sets. It should be possible, however, to set up a brief general strengthening and conditioning program with weights that could be used, at least for preconditioning, by *any* athlete. For that matter, such a program could be used *to keep from getting out of condition* by any *ex*-athlete!

Because there is no better exercise for development of the deltoids and arms, and because it is practiced by all successful weight-trained athletes, the press heads the list. In placing it first, it becomes a warm-up as well as a developer, so it is advisable to lower the weight below the knees after each press, making the exercise a repetition clean and press, rather than just an overhead pushing movement. The cleans help bring into play all the body's muscles, thus stepping up the circulatory and respiratory systems more vigorously. A second exercise, practiced almost universally by successful athletes in varying sports, is the full knee bend, or squat. It is always advisable to follow squats with a light, straight-arm pullover, emphasizing full inhalation and exhalation as the weight is lowered and pulled over the chest. This helps the breathing return to normal, and also results in development of a full, rounded rib cage. These three

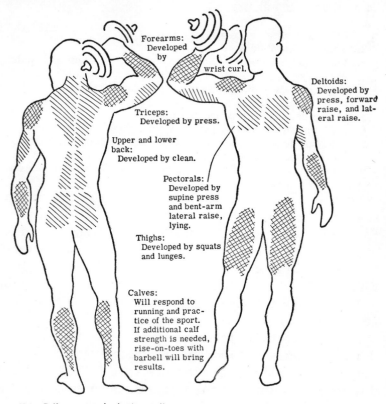

Forearms:
Developed
by
wrist curl.

Deltoids:
Developed by
press, forward
raise, and lateral raise.

Triceps:
Developed by press.

Upper and lower
back:
Developed by clean.

Pectorals:
Developed by
supine press
and bent-arm
lateral raise,
lying.

Thighs:
Developed by squats
and lunges.

Calves:
Will respond to
running and practice of the sport.
If additional calf
strength is needed,
rise-on-toes with
barbell will bring
results.

Note: Pullover expands chest capacity.

Figure 45. Muscles especially valuable in fencing.

exercises will produce good results in conditioning, but several optional movements also should be included if time and facilities permit.

A recommended general strengthening and conditioning program follows in outline form. The optional exercises are those affecting major muscle groups and are the ones most popular with men enjoying practical success:

ATHLETES' GENERAL WEIGHT TRAINING PROGRAM

1. Clean and press, ten repetitions.
2. Full knee bend (squat), fifteen repetitions.
3. Pullover, ten-fifteen repetitions (light weight).

OPTIONAL EXERCISES

4. Alternate press with dumbbells, ten repetitions, each arm.
5. Sit-up with weight behind head, fifteen-twenty repetitions.
6. Curl, ten repetitions
7. Supine press on bench, ten repetitions.
8. Rowing exercise, leaning forward, ten repetitions.
9. Wrestler's bridge with weight held on chest, ten repetitions.

The above are all barbell exercises with the exception of the alternate press, which requires dumbbells. This exercise may be omitted if dumbbell handles are not available, but the inconvenience of loading dumbbells to heavy poundages should not be a reason for neglecting this exercise. Alternate dumbbell pressing has the advantage of allowing the athlete to work his arms and shoulders with considerable speed, yet with quite heavy weights. The exercise also strengthens the side muscles of the torso. Alternate pressing is performed by cleaning two moderately heavy dumbbells to the shoulders and then pushing them to full lock overhead in a see-saw action, one coming down as the other goes up. (*See* Figure 46.) The pressing should be accompanied by a rocking motion of the body.

Any competent coach should be able to make valuable use of weight training by studying the action of his players' bodies in specific sports, and then selecting resistance exercises which strengthen the muscle groups involved. The routines outlined in this book should not be considered the "last word," for there is no reason why coaches everywhere cannot add to knowledge of strengthening and conditioning by devising practical new exercises and variations of old ones.

For the most part, however, unless specific weaknesses are apparent, a balanced program to develop overall strength should add to the performance of any athlete.

Figure 46. Alternate press.

In the routines in this section, listing exercises for specific repetitions, not noting definite progression, or not listing repetitions, the instructor can work from five to eight for power and from eight to twelve for greater endurance with strength. It is not always wise to have everyone working on the same number of repetitions, since different body types respond differently to the exercises. The athlete can often help the instructor by telling him which system of repetitions "feels" as though it is bringing results. If repetitions are cut to five, however, the exercise should be repeated in two to four sets. Whenever the repetitions are completed easily, the weight should be increased.

References

(I) Books

(1) Chandler, Otis, *Scientific Weightlifting Exercises Designed for Track and Field Events.* Mimeographed at the *Los Angeles Times* office and distributed by the author.

(2) Johnson, David G. and Oscar Heidenstam, *Modern Bodybuilding.* London: Faber and Faber Ltd., 1955.

(3) Murray, Jim, *Weight Lifting and Progressive Resistance Exercise.* New York: A. S. Barnes and Company, 1954.

(II) Periodicals

(1) "Barbells Aid Olympic Swimming Aspirants," *Strength and Health,* p. 32, November, 1951.

(2) Bruce, George R., "Mal Whitfield, Iron-Muscled Running Champion," *Strength and Health,* p. 8, December, 1954.

(3) ——, "Parry O'Brien, Shotput Champion," *Strength and Health,* p. 10, August, 1954.

(4) Donelan, Paul F., "Baseball Star Says Weight Training Helps," *Strength and Health,* p. 10, August, 1955.

(5) Drohan, John, "Weight-Lifting Saved Jensen's Arm," *Boston Traveler,* 1955.

(6) Farbotnik, John, "Weight Training Program of Fortune Gordien," *Strength and Health,* p. 10, January, 1954.

(7) Ferguson, Fraysher, "Otis Chandler—Shot Put Champion," *Strength and Health,* p. 22, September, 1952.

(8) ——, "The Cleveland Comet," *Strength and Health,* p. 32, November, 1951.

(9) Goellner, William, "Aggie Weight Star Credits Barbells for Improvement," *Strength and Health,* p. 10, March, 1955.

(10) McCloy, C. H., "Weight Training for Athletes," *Strength and Health,* p. 8, July, 1955.

(11) Murray, Jim, "Barbell Man Sets World Record for 35-pound Weight Throw," *Strength and Health,* p. 14, May, 1954.

(12) ——, "British Speedster Uses Weight Training," *Strength and Health,* p. 11, March, 1955.

(13) ——, "Stan Jones, All-America Football Star," *Strength and Health,* p. 10, August, 1954.

(14) ——, "Summer Training for Football—With Barbells," *Strength and Health,* p. 8, June, 1955.

(15) ——, "Training Schedule of Rev. Bob Richards," *Strength and Health,* p. 10, July, 1952.

Part V

Part V

Chapter 13

Weight Lifting in Competition

IN United States AAU and collegiate weight lifting, and in international competition, such as the Olympic Games, there are three lifts used. The rules and equipment are the same the world over, and training techniques are much the same everywhere. Thus, weight lifting competition can be compared with such sports as track and field.

A weight lifter, to be a champion, must be more than a well-muscled man who can grind heavy poundages overhead with strength alone. He must be an athlete in every sense of the word, with coordination, speed, balance, and competitive spirit, in addition to strength. He needs endurance to a lesser degree than men in many sports, but must condition himself to the point that

157

his body is able to recuperate and ready itself for another great explosive effort after only a short rest.

The first requirement for weight lifting competition is the equipment. The actual lifting takes place on a platform 4 meters square. This approximately 12-feet square platform must be rugged enough to withstand the impact of dropped barbells after missed lifts, so is usually constructed of two layers of heavy boards, with the boards in one layer running perpendicular to those in the other layer. The barbell handle, which the athletes grasp, is $1\frac{1}{10}$ inches in diameter, but is covered by a revolving sleeve at the ends where the weights are attached. The over-all length of the bar is 7 feet, with the length of the portion that can be held (between the inside collars) varying in length from 46 to as much as 52 inches in some European sets.

The weights used to vary the poundage lifted are disc-shaped, and the largest size allowed in standard lifting has a diameter of $17\frac{3}{4}$ inches. In the United States, Great Britain, and many other countries (where American and British sets are used), the largest discs, or plates, weigh 45 pounds, which is also the weight of the bar. Thus, a barbell composed of the bar and two largest standard plates weighs 135 pounds. With outside collars holding the plates in place, the weight would be increased to 145 pounds, the collars weighing 5 pounds each. In Europe, sets are made up in kilos, with the largest plates and bar weighing 44 pounds each. Plates made in the U.S. and Britain are graduated downward, in pounds, as follows: 35, 25, 10, 5, and $2\frac{1}{2}$. In Europe, the smaller plates are 33, 22, 11, $5\frac{1}{2}$, and $2\frac{1}{4}$.

To pass on the correctness of each lift, there are three officials, a referee and two judges. In case of disagreement on the passability of a lift, majority rules, with the referee's vote counting no more than the judges'. In the case of a world record, however, the lift must be approved unanimously. The referee's responsibilities include more than deciding the correctness of the lift, since in each lift he decides when the athlete has the barbell correctly under control and signals when the weight may be lowered. The referee also signals when the lifter may begin to press in the first of the three lifts. The signal given to start a press is a clap of the hands. The signal given to lower a completed lift is a downward wave of the hand, usually with a spoken "down." Many referees signal that the weight may be lowered by a sharp hand clap, followed by a shout of "down" and a wave of the hand, to be sure that the lifter understands. The signal must be obvious, especially when an audience is applauding a good lift.

Clothing worn by competitors is usually trunks and T-shirt. Regular gym shoes are used by competitors using the "split style" of lifting, to be described, and shoes with higher heels are worn by men using the "squat style." Regular warm-up suits, usually called sweat suits, are worn during training periods, but during competition the legs and arms must be uncovered, and shirts must be snug fitting in order to facilitate judging.

Some lifters wear heavy belts, which afford some support to the small of the back, but international rules limit the width of belts to four inches.

There are three standard tests of combined strength and athletic ability in weight lifting, called the press, snatch, and clean and jerk. These will be dealt with separately. Each competitor is allowed three attempts in each lift, or nine lifts in a contest. If a first attempt is successful, the lifter must increase the weight of the barbell by at least 10 pounds for his second try. He is not limited to 10 pounds, however, but may increase as much over the minimum as he chooses. If his second attempt is successful he must increase at least 5 pounds, but is not limited to this amount, for his third try. A competitor who feels he has started too high after making his first lift may, if successful, increase only 5 pounds for his second attempt, but by so doing forfeits his third attempt.

If a lifter is unsuccessful with his first or second attempts, he may repeat them with the same weight. If he is attempting to set a record and is unsuccessful in three tries, he may be granted up to ten attempts by the officials, but the extra tries for a record may not be counted in his total. A lifter is allowed three minutes rest between attempts, providing that much time has not been taken up by the lifting of his competitors. He may lift before three minutes has elapsed, however.

The totals made by competitors on their best successful press, snatch, and clean and jerk determine the winners in the seven bodyweight classes contested in the United States and internationally. In case of a tie, the lighter man wins. The bodyweight classes are as follows:

> 123¼ pounds—Bantamweight
> 132¼ pounds—Featherweight
> 148¾ pounds—Lightweight
> 165¼ pounds—Middleweight
> 181¾ pounds—Lightheavyweight
> 198¼ pounds—Middleheavyweight
> Over 198¼ pounds—Heavyweight

Most American weight lifting competition occurs in meets organized by the Amateur Athletic Union of the United States. There are, however, team contests between colleges and intercollegiate meets open to men from NCAA schools. To get the "feel" of an actual contest, the budding lifter should attend meets as a spectator. This will give him an idea how much he should be able to lift in order to have a chance of competing on even terms with the place-winners. As a general rule, however, a man able to lift a barbell approximately equal to his own weight in the press, and snatch, and about 50 pounds more in the clean and jerk, is ready to compete in most district contests. AAU competition includes Novice, Junior, and Senior, or Open, meets. Open meets may be entered by any registered AAU athlete, providing he shows a proper travel permit if from out of the district. Senior meets may be entered by any AAU athlete in the district. Junior meets may be entered by any district AAU athlete who has not won a junior or senior meet previously.

Novice meets are open to anyone who has never won a previous novice contest or been a medalist in more advanced competition.

Information about securing Amateur Athletic Union membership can be obtained by writing to the national headquarters at 233 Broadway, New York City.

The two-arms press

There are three standard lifts used internationally, so they will be described in the order followed in competition. First is the press, which the rules state must be done as follows: The barbell must be pulled (cleaned) to the shoulders or upper chest in a single motion, starting from a position horizontally in front of the lifter's legs. As long as the pull to the chest is not interrupted, splitting, dipping, or squatting under the barbell is permitted. Before beginning the overhead portion of the lift, however, the legs must be straight (knees locked), the feet on the same line and no farther than (approximately) 16 inches apart. The referee determines that the lifter is standing erect with the weight at his chest with the legs in position as described before clapping his hands to signal that the weight may be pushed (pressed) overhead.

A jerk, or obvious sudden start, is forbidden at the start of the press overhead. While pressing, the lifter must stand erect in the position he assumed with the weight at his chest. He is not permitted to look up at the bar as it travels to arms' length. Causes for disqualification include: raising of the heels or toes (loss of balance), obvious body sway (extreme back bend), lowering the barbell before pressing, and any heaving of the barbell at the start. The barbell may not stop in its upward progress, may not be pressed unevenly (one end higher than the other), and the lifter is not permitted any obvious twisting of his body.

If a lifter is, for any reason, unable to rest the bar on his chest before pressing, he should so inform the referee. Here again the rule applies—the barbell may not be lowered to obtain a rebound.

So much for the rules.

Before actually pressing the weight overhead, the lifter must pull the barbell to his shoulders. This will cause most men little difficulty, especially when first learning the lift, but it is wise to learn to make the clean with an economy of effort in order to conserve strength for the press. The lifter should set himself carefully to clean for the press, even though he knows he can pull the weight to the shoulders easily. His feet should be under the barbell, so that when the lowers his hips to grasp the bar his shins actually brush it. A straight-back pulling position is important, and the hands should hold the barbell firmly, but without unnatural squeezing. The arms should be straight and almost relaxed at the start of the pull, done by beginning to straighten the legs. As the barbell reaches knee height, the leg drive continues and the arms and back are brought into strong action. The barbell is whipped over to the chest with a quick rise-on-toes, then a slight dip of the knees and snap of the wrists. As the weight strikes the chest, the lifter sets himself solidly with feet in comfortable position and knees locked.

Some lifters may develop pressing power out of proportion to their pull, and in this case will want to "split" in getting the weight to the shoulders. In this case it is wise to keep one foot stationary (usually the left foot in right-handed men) and step back with the other while lowering the body by bending the stationary leg. If this is done the feet should be brought back on the same line as quickly as possible in order to assume correct pressing position while holding the weight for as short a time as possible. Holding the weight at the chest for more than the required two seconds is often the final straw that stops a limit press from going up.

Most men, however, will find that their pull will be adequate to catch the barbell chest-high by merely dipping slightly at the knees.

The man who is easily able to clean weights that he can press, without moving his feet, will be wise to set his feet in the position he has found most comfortable and efficient for a solid pressing stance. Often this will mean that the feet will be spaced slightly wider than when the first consideration is limit pulling ability, as in the snatch or the clean for the jerk.

To digress for a moment, it should be mentioned that some men press with what is called a "thumbless grip." This means that the thumb is behind the bar with the fingers, instead of wrapped around. This makes the grip slightly weaker in cleaning, but seldom so much so as to bother a lifter. Those who favor the thumbless grip say it enables them to concentrate their strength into an upward drive, rather than have some strength wasted in gripping the bar tightly with the thumbs. At the opposite extreme, some men feel that their grip needs reinforcing for the clean, and use what is known as the "hook." This means that the thumb is placed *around* the bar and then encircled by the first, or the first and second fingers as the hand takes hold. This grip is recommended for the snatch and clean, but few men will need it when pressing. When hooking, a lifter has an almost fool-proof hold on the bar without tense squeezing, thus it is valuable in heavy upward pulls.

With the barbell at the chest, the lifter should set himself as quickly as possible to start pressing, because in actual practice most referees will give the starting clap as soon as the lifter is settled and ready, rather than arbitrarily counting two seconds from the time the bar strikes his chest.

Every man will have to experiment with varying hand spacing and "drives" overhead to find the style best suited to him. In fact, most good lifters, in action for a number of years, vary fine points in their styles from time to time. For most men, however, a hand spacing slightly wider than the lifter's shoulders will be about right. Individual leverage will cause some men to evolve to a spacing considerably wider and others to press as close as with the hands touching the deltoid muscles, though this latter is not recommended because it often leads to excessive back bend, and results in disqualification.

A solid stance is vital to make a heavy press. (*See* Figure 47.) The legs should be held straight forcibly and the hips locked, with pelvis thrust forward slightly. This position means that the lifter will start pressing with his body bowed forward. He should carry through with this position in that his head should be held back as much as possible without actually looking up. In this locked, arched position, it is possible to press the barbell in almost a straight line upward to arms' length. The advantage to

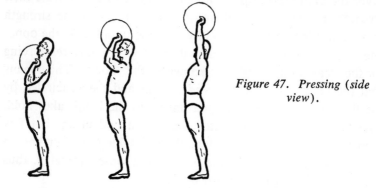

Figure 47. Pressing (side view).

a straight-line press lies in the fact that the lifter is able to concentrate on an all-out drive. If the barbell should get away from this vertical direction, especially if it is pushed out over the lifter's toes, the deltoids will be called upon to compensate and bring it back and will no longer be pressing upward. When the barbell is improperly pushed too far forward, it also results in a compensating back bend which is often so pronounced as to cause disqualification.

The press should begin from a point on the upper chest near the clavicle. The lower the barbell can be held comfortably at the start, the more muscle drive it will be possible to place behind the lift. A strong drive is important. At one time, officials required that the barbell move slowly, keeping pace with the referee's slowly-rising hand, but this is no longer required. As long as there is no starting jerk, the press may be as fast as the lifter can make it. The lifter, therefore, should take advantage of this liberalization of the rules and really ram the barbell upward. Obviously the weight of a limit poundage will restrict the speed of the barbell sufficiently to make the lift a true press.

Figure 48. Pressing (front view).

One method of giving the weight a fast start, which is acceptable if done smoothly, is as follows: The lifter cleans the barbell high on his chest to a point he has found to be about an inch higher than the point from which he can press most strongly. He then allows the weight to settle slowly, so that the lowering is imperceptible, and times it so that the weight reaches his efficient starting point just as the starting signal is given. He then drives the weight up as close to is face as possible. (*See* Figure 48.) Some good lifters have timed a sharp inhalation to coincide with the starting drive, so as to be pressing on full lungs, but most men inhale fully as soon as the weight strikes the chest and hold the lungs full throughout the press. As long as this slight slump and drive is not too obvious, the lifter will not be disqualified.

The lifter should endeavor to maintain his starting position as closely as possible throughout the press and to hold it at the conclusion. Some outstanding lifters, however, press with the slight body arch described, but shift their bodies forward under the weight, as it passes their heads, to finish in a more erect position with the barbell directly overhead. Movement of this kind, however, should be held to a minimum.

Another style of pressing in vogue with "natural" pressers, men with good leverage and unusually strong deltoids, involves a more exaggerated arch, with the chest held high and the hands gripping the barbell several inches wider than the shoulders. In this style, the arch is very obvious, and it would be grounds for disqualification to straighten at the completion of the press. The arch is not cause for disqualification, as officiating has evolved in recent years, as long as the same position is held throughout the press, and the lifter does not lean so far as to actually look up at the barbell at the finish.

When pressing with a wide grip, most lifters take a full breath on hearing the starting signal and hold it throughout the effort. With a very wide grip, the hands will be more comfortable with thumbs around the bar.

A closer grip permits more of a jolt in the starting drive, but once the barbell is moving in a wide-grip style, it is easier to keep it going and finish the lift. A number of record-holders have used this wide grip style with success, with 1953 world heavyweight champion Doug Hepburn, of Canada, and 1946 world lightheavyweight champion Gregory Novak, of Russia, especially notable. Hepburn, who stood 69 inches tall and weighed approximately 300 pounds, succeeded with a world record of 381 pounds using the lay back, wide grip style. Hepburn was one of the few men limited, in his press, to the weight he could pull to his shoulders, having disproportionate strength in pushing heavy poundages overhead. Novak was able to exert his strength to better advantage in pulling, but his heavily muscled 180 to 190 pounds at less than 64 inches in height was unusually well-suited to pressing overhead. Using slightly less body arch than Hepburn, but also with a wide grip, Novak set world records of 315½ as a lightheavyweight and a pound more in the mid-heavy division.

Equally meritorious presses have been made with more erect stance and nearer shoulder width grip by such men as Tommy Kono, U.S. lifter who won world championships in three classes. As a middleweight, Kono set a world mark of 288¾ pounds, and weighing only 170 pounds he exceeded the heavier Novak's record with a press of 316¼. Paul Anderson, with his hands spaced just outside his shoulders, pressed 409 pounds officially, maintaining an erect position, with only enough arch to get the weight past his face. Anderson was the same height as Hepburn and weighed 331½ pounds when he made the lift.

An unusually close pressing grip was used by U.S. heavyweight champion Steve Stanko when he became the first man in the world officially to total 1,000 pounds on the standard lifts (1941). Stanko, a 71½-inch athlete weighing 225 pounds, actually rested his hands on his broad shoulders at the start of the press. This meant he was holding the barbell at the very inner edge of the knurled handgrips, a distance of only 15 inches between his hands. He officially pressed 310 pounds with this style, which closely approached the world record at the time, but his narrow grip had the disadvantage of causing him to lean away from the weight if he should be having one of the "off days" known to even the greatest of athletes at times.

It is interesting to note the instruction given by respected coaches on correct pressing. Bob Hoffman, most prominent U.S. coach, says the press should be done with elbows consciously held in. Other points emphasized by Hoffman are keeping the weight close to the face, and getting it back over the head as quickly as possible (as mentioned previously, a method used by many Russian lifters who shift forward under the barbell as it goes up).

A keen analyst of lifting styles, British National and Olympic Coach Al Murray emphasizes that the lifter should find a position with the chest high, head back (but not looking up), and thighs and hips thrust forward. This, Murray has found through observation and practice, brings the barbell, hip joints, and insteps in a vertical line through a common center of gravity. He advises that the barbell should be pressed vertically (not forward) off the chest with "great fierceness," and that the lifter attempt to hold his chest high throughout the effort. Murray has found, as will all lifters practicing this strength test, that the most difficult stage of the lift occurs as the barbell passes the athlete's nose and continues the few inches needed to clear his head. This peak resistance results from the most unfavorable leverage during the lift, or as Murray says, "due to the horizontal distance between the weight and shoulders being at its greatest." If the weight feels forward as it passes the top of the head, probably the fault most often causing failure with limit attempts, Murray suggests the lifter "ease the thighs slightly forward and lift the chest as high as possible" while continuing to press strongly. This, he has concluded, will bring the lifter back into balance, to the line of least resistance, or the "groove" in which the maximum muscle force can be exerted most efficiently.

A number of sound observations on this apparently simple, but difficult-in-practice lift have been made by Harry B. Paschall, a former United States middleweight champion and popular writer on the subject. Paschall says, "There is one basic point in making a good press; the hip-lock. Unless the legs are locked, braced, tied-in with the locking of the lower back and hips, you have not the correct foundation to press upon. If you put your feet too wide apart you are not going to get this lock; and at the moment you need the firmly braced back most, you are going to weaken into a backbend." Paschall suggests that the barbell be cleaned higher than necessary, with a strong pull, and recommends a grip wider than the shoulders. Before pressing, Paschall says, ". . . the arms are relaxed, the bell rests across the clavicular joint, a deep breath is taken, and the bell is started easily upward, gaining in momentum as it reaches the eyes. The head must be kept back and the bar pressed with a feeling of grazing the nose, as CLOSE in as possible, so that when the bell reaches the top of the head, you can get it directly overhead and finish the press."

Perhaps the gaining-in-momentum after an "easy start" might better be described as fighting hard to keep the barbell moving faster after it leaves the chest. Most outstanding lifters make every effort to give the weight a strong start. An attempt to place too much starting drive behind a press, however, can result in the barbell being "thrown away" forward. This places too much strain on the deltoids and invariably results in leaning back to compensate and keep the weight moving. The correct drive is described by Paschall as, ". . . you throw all of your power into the upward movement, trying to force the bar slightly back, close to the face, and seeking the 'groove'. . . ."

The preparation for lifting limit weights in competition is done by practicing the lift itself in sets of low repetitions, working up in poundage. It is not wise to work to an all-out effort every training period, and experienced lifters will learn to gauge their work output by their feelings and the length of time it takes them to recover to full strength after limit exercise. For the man wanting to increase his training poundages gradually and regularly, while not able to accurately predict on which days he is ready to "shoot the works," a schedule based on percentages can be used. Following such a schedule can help remove an ever-present temptation to try limit lifting every training day. Too much limit work tends to hold an athlete at a static level. This is probably due, for the most part, to the fact that the athlete's rest between workouts is not sufficient to allow him to recuperate adequately from lifting to the limit of his strength and nervous energy.

A suggested schedule of percentage increases for three training days per week is as follows:

Monday:

After warming up with several repetition cleans and presses using a light barbell, press 70 per cent of limit three repetitions; 80 per cent three repetitions; 85 to 90 per cent of limit three sets of three repetitions.

Wednesday:

Warm up and then press 75 per cent of limit three repetitions; 80 per cent three repetitions; 85 per cent three repetitions; 90 to 95 per cent of limit three sets of *two* repetitions.

Friday (or Saturday):

Warm up and then press 75 per cent of limit three repetitions; 85 per cent three repetitions; 90 per cent two repetitions; and work up in three single presses from 95 to 102½ per cent of limit.

Obviously it will not be possible to reach 102½ per cent of limit in each lift every time the attempt is made, but whenever progress is registered, the entire schedule should be re-figured on a basis of the new personal record. There are days when weight lifters will not feel up to a limit effort. If this is due to illness, of course, the workout should be skipped altogether, but if it is just a case of feeling "a bit under par," the poundages lifted should be moderated.

There are other possible training schedules, but the percentage system described above (which also will be discussed for training on the snatch, and clean and jerk) was used with success by John Terpak, assistant U.S. Olympic coach, while instructing a group of Mexican lifters. Terpak, himself a member of two Olympic teams and twice a world champion, helped improve the standard of weight lifting in Mexico while coaching as a guest of the Mexican government.

Another system of training for the press is to warm up and then work up in a series of three repetition presses in 20-pound jumps to a weight approximately 25 pounds below the lifter's best single press. Then 10 pounds is added to the barbell (to 15 pounds below limit) for eight to ten single presses. For example, if the lifter's best press is 200 pounds, he would work up as follows:

Three presses with 135 pounds, three presses with 155 pounds, three presses with 175 pounds, and then eight to ten single presses with 185 pounds.

Other lifters have worked up to a series of two presses with a given weight, moving the weight up 5 or 10 pounds on the barbell every third or fourth workout. For the man pressing 200 pounds at best, a sample workout might go as follows:

Three presses with 135 pounds, three presses with 155 pounds, and then six to eight sets of two repetition presses with 180 pounds.

There are many good "assistance" exercises which aid in developing pressing power and incidentally add variety to training. Assistance exercises are those which strengthen specific muscle groups used in the competitive lifts. To boost pressing power, two of the best exercises are the simultaneous press with two dumbbells, and the supine press on bench with barbell. It should be noted at this point that while working the leg and back muscles hard on successive days will almost always provide more work than the body's rebuilding process can take care of to advantage, pressing exercises can often be done on one or two "off" days with good results.

One system of "off-day training" is to press dumbbells simultaneously, several sets of three to five repetitions. (*See* Figure 49.) Using the limit 200-pound press example again, the lifter could press dumbbells, weighing 70 pounds each, four sets of five repetitions. Or he could press 75-pound dumbbells five sets of four repetitions, or 80-pound dumbbells six sets of three repetitions. Note that the recommended *total* number of repetitions is eighteen to twenty. Dumbbell pressing has been used effectively on Tuesdays and Thursdays by lifters following regular Monday-Wednesday-Friday workouts.

Another system of off-day pressing is to use a barbell taken from the stands ordinarily used to shoulder a weight for squatting. This eliminates cleaning entirely, confining the action primarily to the shoulders and arms. A workable system of pressing from stands is to start with four sets of three repetitions, working up, with a normal hand spacing. Then three sets of three with the hands spaced several inches wider than normal, again working up, but from about 20 pounds lower starting point. To finish the workout, three more sets of three are done using a narrower hand spacing. This will permit more weight to be used than the wide grip, but less than the normal grip. Weight increases should be 10 pounds per set. Most men will find they will get good results with this routine without working any higher than 30 pounds below their best press, even with the normal hand spacing.

Figure 49. Simultaneous press with two dumbbells.

The supine press with barbell is used by many champion lifters *after* completing a regular Monday-Wednesday-Friday session of lifting. This exercise can be used to advantage in accustoming the arm extensor muscles to handling heavier weights than can be pressed overhead standing. A weight should be used which is at least 10 pounds heavier than the lifter's best overhead press, and five sets of three repetition supine presses is recommended. For men who find themselves able to press heavy weights in the supine position, it is advisable to increase the weight of the barbell 10 pounds after each set of presses. Occasionally it is a good idea to work to a single limit supine press. This will help develop great pressing strength and has the psychological effect of making the lifter believe the weight he is pressing overhead is actually "light."

When practicing the supine press, the lifter should have two training partners hand him the weight either at the position from which he presses at the chest or at arms' length over the chest. The assistants should stand by to remove the barbell after the presses are completed, or to catch it and lift it off the exerciser if he is unable to complete a press. As an assistance exercise, the supine press will bring better results if the same hand spacing is used on the barbell as when pressing overhead.

THE PRESS, SUMMARY

1. Clean with a strong, high pull and get set quickly.
2. Press with all the drive possible, and keep driving as though to speed the upward movement of the weight.
3. Press *back* from the chest, close to the face and head.
4. Maintain starting position with legs and hips tensed and pelvis thrust forward; hold chest high throughout press.
5. Hold position with weight at locked arms (Do not sway forward.) until referee signals "down."

The two-arms snatch

The second standard weight lifting test is one of the most complicated athletic feats, though its rules seem quite simple. Basically it is an "all pull" lift. The rules state that the barbell must be lifted from a position horizontally in front of the lifter's legs to fully locked arms overhead in a single, uninterrupted motion. The lifter is permitted to lower himself under the barbell to any extent short of touching a knee to the floor, providing the upward motion of the weight is not interrupted. Causes for disqualification include: touching a knee to the floor, a break (known as "press-out") in the upward motion, failure to bring the lift under control within the limits of the standard platform, and failure to hold the barbell overhead while standing erect for the two-second count and referee's signal of approval.

There are two distinct styles used in snatching, but a beginner learning the lift will be wise to concern himself with neither at the start, first learning the basic all-the-way-up pull without thinking about getting under the weight as it rises. The pull is as follows: The lifter stands close to the barbell, so close that when he reaches down to grasp it his shins brush (or almost brush) the handle. The entire pull should be made as close to the legs and body as possible, starting from the floor. The bar should be grasped with the palms toward the lifter, using a hand-spacing wider than that for the press. In other words, the average grip for snatching is considerably wider than the width of the shoulders.

Gripping the barbell firmly, but not squeezing (the hook grip is recommended), the lifter lowers his hips and raises his head so that his back flattens, with hips lower than shoulders, immediately before the pull is started. Thus the initial impetus comes from the legs and back, with the arms hanging almost relaxed. As the barbell reaches knee height, it is pulled in close to the thighs, and the back and arms follow through and attempt to accelerate the upward motion. The legs will fully straighten, the hips thrust forward and up as a final leg "kick" is delivered by a quick rise-on-toes. At this point, the barbell is whipped over by the wrists, and the arms are rammed to full lock with the weight overhead. For this learning motion, a slight dip of the knees will be the only concession made in lowering under the weight. This exercise, often termed the "flip snatch," will teach the lifter to make full use of his pulling power to get weights overhead. Practiced in sets of three to five repetitions, with as much weight as possible, it is a fine exercise to develop pulling strength.

Once a good pull is developed, with a quick follow-through to solid arm-lock, the lifter should experiment with the two styles of lifting, the "split" and the "squat." In the split, the lifter lowers himself under the barbell by lunging under the weight as it reaches the limit to which it can be pulled, assuming a position similar to that of a fencer delivering an all-out thrust. One leg is back in an on-toe position, and the other leg (usually the left in right-handed men) is bent, with knee ahead of ankle, and preferably with the hip lower than the knee.

In the squat, the lifter lowers himself under the barbell by jumping his feet apart for balance and "sitting down" into a full knee bend to catch the weight overhead. In both styles, the lift must be completed by standing erect with the weight overhead and under control, and with the feet on the same line.

In detail, the split style (*See* Figure 50.) is as follows: The barbell is pulled up exactly as described for the flip snatch exercise, starting with hips low, head up, and back flat. With a limit weight, it will be impossible to pull the barbell all the way overhead, so the lifter lunges under it as it passes chest height. Actually the lifter must learn to feel when he has exerted his absolute limit in pull and must move under the weight at that split second—not before and not after it. If he splits too soon, the barbell will have insufficient impetus for him to catch it at locked arms, even in the lowest split position. If he splits too late, gravity will have overcome the impetus of his pull, and the barbell will be on its way down before he can get under it.

When splitting, the feet leave the floor in a front and back direction with the final rise-on-toes of the pull. Since the final whip of the pull at its height is back, the back foot will travel farther in almost every case. The front step action is important, however, to cock the leg with knee ahead of ankle, in order to drop into the low position. As the feet hit the floor, the lifter should have his hands turned over and be ramming to a complete lock while continuing to lower the body by bending the front leg. The final position should be solid, with the barbell overhead, the arms locked, the front leg in a position similar to a one-legged squat, and the rear leg extended to an almost straight position, though slightly bent for control and stability.

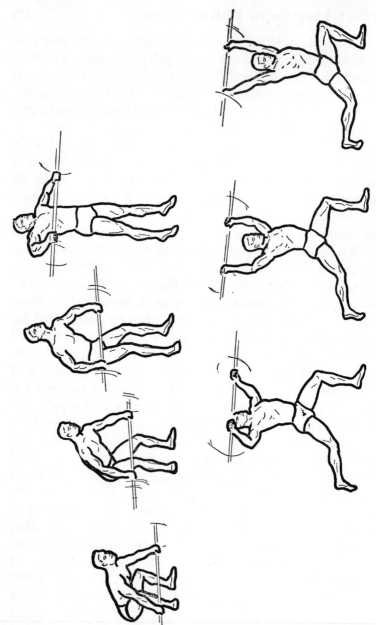

Figure 50. *Two arms snatch (split style).*

When pulling preparatory to splitting, it is important that the pull be continued all the way to the kick off of the rise-on-toes, at which point the feet leave the floor in opposite directions. A common fault is to take the rear foot off the floor first. This can have three bad effects on the lift: (1) The end of the barbell on the side toward the rear foot will not be pulled as high as the other end, resulting in a one-arm press-out. (2) The overall pull will be weakened so that the barbell will not reach sufficient height to complete the lift. (3) The premature picking up of the rear foot will accentuate the step back to the point that the barbell will be too far in front, even though at arms' length, to be held overhead under control.

Each lifter should experiment with varying hand spacing. The wider the hands are placed, the less distance the weight needs to be pulled. The closer the spacing, however, the more assistance that can be added to the pull by the arm and shoulder muscles. With a relatively wide grip, the barbell can be "caught" at the height of the pull with less emphasis on ramming the arms to a locked-out position. With a closer grip, however, many lifters have learned to coordinate a pull-push action which does not violate the rule that states the barbell must keep moving upward constantly. With this method, the lifter pulls hard, lunges, and turns his hands over to push the barbell to locked arms, at the same time continuing to drop lower in the split. When the push is for a short distance, made quickly and completed at the same time the body reaches the lowest position, there is no apparent press-out.

A close grip cannot be used effectively in the squat snatch, however, since consistent success with this method requires that the shoulders be rotated backward as the low position is reached. The shoulders can only be rotated backward properly if the hands are considerably more than shoulder width apart on the bar.

The squatter will be wise to experiment to determine the narrowest comfortable grip he can use. Because of the need to get the shoulders back, this will not be very narrow. In fact, most men of average height, or more, hold within an inch or two of the collars, or solidly against them. The starting pull for the squat snatch (*See* Figure 51.) is the same as for the "flip" or split; hips low, head up, and back flat. As the pull is exhausted, however, the lifter jumps his feet apart at the conclusion of the final rise-on-toes, then plants them solidly as he "sits down" under the weight. In learning the form, the lifter can work down deeper and deeper into the squat by increasing the weight until he has to hit "bottom" to catch it at arms' length.

Larry Barnholth, an outstanding coach at the American College of Modern Weight Lifting in Akron, Ohio, advises that the lifter drive upward out of the squat position as soon as the barbell is at locked arms. Some men, however, hold the full squat momentarily to attain solid balance. At the low squat position, the head should be thrust forward and the arms and shoulders rolled back. The forward head position compresses the trapezius against the backward-held deltoids, giving a solid base for holding the weight overhead. Each individual will have to experiment until he finds his own best "angles" of forward lean and arms back. Barnholth advises a 45-degree forward tilt of the back. While starting to rise, the head should be held forward, but once the lifter is part way up, he can gradually look more directly ahead without losing control. Looking up while in the low position tends to relax the shoulders and spoil a solidly balanced position, resulting in the barbell being dropped.

Squat style lifters will find higher-than-normal heels an advantage in reaching a comfortable position. One and one-half to two-inch heels are often used on regular street shoes (or high ankled "work shoes") with non-skid soles, or they can be attached to regular gym shoes.

There has been considerable disagreement among leading coaches about the direction of pull in snatching (and cleaning, which will be discussed later). Bob Hoffman instructs lifters to pull the barbell straight up to the limit of their pulling ability

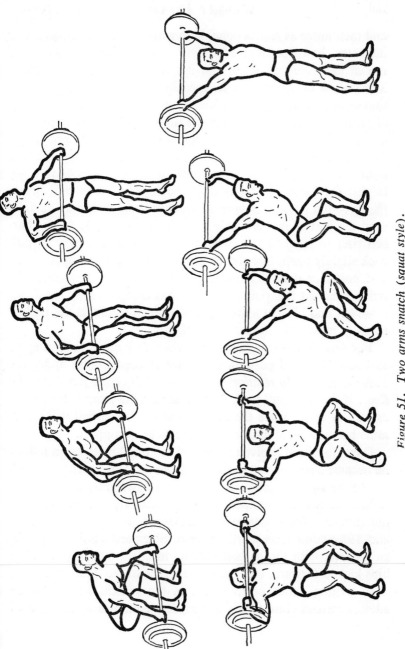

Figure 51. Two arms snatch (squat style).

and then move as fast as possible in getting under it. Observation indicates, however, that a straight-up pull does not make full use of the lifter's muscles, and is not used in the literal sense. The pull is fairly straight to knee height, but must be back at that point to keep the weight close, and in the most efficient zone of muscle force. Once in over the thighs, inertia has been overcome by the initial leg and back drive, and the arms, upper back, and shoulders come into play on what is, in effect, a *lighter* weight because of its upward motion. Once over the thighs, the "kicking" forward of the hips and arm pull brings the direction back near vertical (and in some men may actually send the barbell momentarily away from the lifter). As the barbell rises in front of the chest, however, it is necessary to pull back slightly again in order to get the full use of the upper back and posterior deltoid muscles, as well as to begin turning the wrists over. At this point, the lifter has completed his leg drive, however, and his feet leave the floor, which results in the barbell actually moving backward only slightly.

For this reason squatters are advised to jump their feet apart and seek the solid position they have learned to find under the barbell, *moving in relation to the barbell once the feet leave the floor*. If the final pull back is pronounced, the jump will be back as well as apart, since the lifter's hold on the barbell will determine his movement after his feet are clear of support.

Dave Sheppard evolved more and more follow-through pull as he became stronger and moved up from the 148- to 165- to 181- to the 198-pound class. At lighter bodyweights, early in his career, he actually jumped forward, then later stayed with the pull longer with a subsequent backward jump as he set 181- and 198-pound class world records. Sheppard said he lifted in an S-curve, with the barbell moving in at the knees, out as the hips kicked forward, and back strongly with the final pull.

In writing about performance of the snatch, Bob Hoffman advises, "Stand close to the weight, feet comfortably apart, with back flat and hips low. Keep arms straight, head up, and start as in the dead lift. Pull high and close to the body. Before splitting, the body should not only be straight, but raised on toes with head back. . . . Pull as high as possible and split as low as possible, moving the feet equally front and back. Have the knee of the front leg well in front of the ankle, so you can rock under the weight if necessary. Most of the weight should be on the front foot. I have always recommended a comparatively close grip in snatching . . . A lifter can pull higher and harder in this position."

Hoffman does not write in any detail about the squat style, which he does not recommend because it is possible to fail on all three attempts due to the balance involved. In the split style, it is necessary to pull higher, but even if off balance, a lifter should be strong enough to hold a weight overhead by "fight," even though he is staggering all over the platform. In the squat, it is necessary to catch the weight in the proper "groove," for if it is too far front or back, it must be dropped. No lifter should fail to experiment with the squat style, however, because of the ease with which heavy weights can be pulled up to locked arms with this method. It might be said that it is easier to lift in the squat style, but easier to recover from the split.

The instruction given by British coach Al Murray for the split snatch is precise and specific. To start, he advises a hand-spacing of approximately 30 inches in gripping the bar, and that the feet be about 12 inches apart. With the insteps under the bar, Murray says the back should be flat, but not vertical; shoulders forward over the bar; head up and eyes looking forward. He advocates a straight-up pull, noting that as the legs are straightened, raising the hips, the knees move back, allowing the bar to move vertically. As the bar is passing the knees, Murray advises lifters to "stay evenly on both feet. Drive the head and chest high, and simultaneously. Thrust the hips viciously upwards and forwards towards the bar. Pull strongly with the arms, making sure the elbows travel sideways. Reach as high as you can on the toes of both feet. . . . As you reach your greatest height on your toes, take both feet off the ground at exactly the same time. Your feet having left the floor, your body will continue to travel forward . . . and under the bar. Owing to the fact that both feet are off the floor and the body is travelling forward, the rear foot should come in contact with the floor first, having the shortest distance to travel, owing to the backward limitation at the hip-joint. The rear leg can now be used to assist the forward hip thrust in driving the body forwards under the bar. (With the barbell past the top of the head) the wrists are now . . . turned over so that the bar can be driven vertically overhead with the heels of the hands, simultaneously the front knee must be pushed forward over the front foot.

"Having pushed the forward knee forward and driven the heels of the hand vertically upwards, the body will now be correctly balanced under the bar, i.e. bar, shoulders, and hip-joints in one vertical line. . . ."

Murray's detailed instruction for recovery from the deep split position is worth noting: "Allow the bar to tip back ever so slightly; immediately straighten both legs. The rear leg will reach extension first; continue to push with the front leg, using the rear leg as a prop; it will then be simple to move the front foot back a few inches. . . . (Then) tip the bar slightly forward and upward and push off with the rear foot, bringing it in line with the front foot. . . ."

As an aid in learning the split snatch, Murray has devised a diagram, which can be painted on the floor of a lifting platform. The diagram, known as the "Murray Cross," (See Figure 52.) is as follows:

If Murray's instruction is followed to the letter, the feet will be in the broad cross piece at the start of the lift, and on either side of the thin cross piece, front and behind the broad section, at the deep split position. The lift would finish with the feet back in the broad section of the cross.

The Murray Cross could also be used by lifters using the split style taught in America to determine the amount of fore and aft foot movement. U.S. Coach Hoffman says the split should be equally front and back in an ideal lift, though he recommends that the feet strike the floor simultaneously.

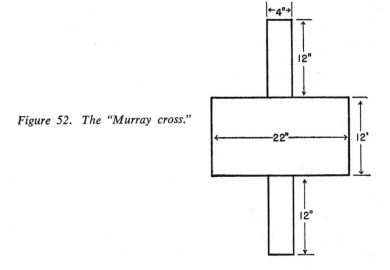

Figure 52. The "Murray cross."

In practice, few lifters step as far front as they do back. This was especially noteworthy in the case of Norbert Schemansky, who set an official world heavyweight record of 334 pounds using the split style. Schemansky's step back was pronounced, but this is not to say that the British style described above is incorrect, however, for Murray has given many personal demonstrations that it is reliable and efficient. On a tour of England, he worked up to 220 pounds on an average of twice a week, while weighing under the middleweight limit. He snatched 180 pounds a total of one hundred and twelve times within a period of forty-five minutes on one occasion, without having one lift go out of control. While this does not compare with Schemansky's regular lifting of 300 pounds or more, the heavyweight champion's great power and athletic ability must be considered. It remains a possibility that Schemansky might have snatched more with the British style, which is certainly worth trying by any lifter endeavoring to improve his snatching ability.

It is obvious from the varying opinions of men who are unquestionably experts on the subject of weight lifting that the barbell will have to travel somewhat differently with relation to different men lifting. Some may make a nearly straight-up pull, others may pull back strongly, and others may get best results by pulling in, up and away, and back again. For sound coaching, however, the following fundamentals should be stressed:

THE SNATCH, SUMMARY

1. The lifter must make the pull as close to himself as possible.
2. Upward acceleration of the barbell from knee height is vital.
3. Complete leg drive up onto the toes is important, in coordination with the final arm pull.
4. All lifters, using split and squat styles, must learn to move with explosive speed and power to get under the weight.

Harry Paschall, himself a split-style snatcher who once held the U.S. middleweight record, became convinced that the squat style was more efficient after seeing the technique developed by coaches Larry, Lewis, and Claude Barnholth and their protégés, such as Pete George. Paschall wrote, "We will readily grant that it will be difficult for older lifters to change to this style; and also, a supremely fast man, like Schemansky for instance, may do almost as well in the split technique. . . . If (the squat snatch) is done correctly . . . it is solid and trustworthy. . . . (The squat snatch has) an easier pull, a much simpler movement all the way. Besides, the bar need not be lifted as high as in the split by several long, long inches."

Larry Barnholth has written, "During a period of over 25 years that I have been coaching lifters I have yet to find a person who could snatch as much in the split style as he could in the squat style after he had learned both methods *correctly*. The reason that the majority of lifters today use the split rather than the squat is that the split style is easier to learn. . . . Anyone can pick up form of one sort or another in split style with little or no teaching."

A system of percentage lifts can be used in snatching as with the press. A practiced method is as follows:

Monday:

After warming up with flip snatches, and by sinking into the deep squat or split position with weight overhead several times, snatch 70 per cent of limit three repetitions; 75 per cent three repetitions; 80 per cent three repetitions; 85 to 90 per cent of limit five to ten single snatches. After the first snatch, succeeding repetitions should be lowered slightly below the knees, to what is termed the "dead hang" position.

Wednesday:

Warm up and then snatch 75 per cent of limit three repetitions; 80 per cent three repetitions; 85 per cent three single snatches; 90 to 95 per cent six single snatches.

Friday (or Saturday):

Warm up and then snatch 75 per cent of limit three repetitions; 85 per cent three repetitions; 90 per cent two single snatches; 95 to 102½ per cent of limit in three single snatches (increasing weight each time).

As in the press, it will not always be possible to work to 102½ per cent of limit on the heavy day. In the snatch, as in the press, there are other systems of working up in training poundage, two of which are outlined below:

Heavy Singles Based on Best Snatch of 200 Pounds:

Three snatches with 135, three snatches with 155, three snatches with 175, and then eight to ten singles with 185.

Heavy Doubles Based on Best Snatch of 200 Pounds:

Three snatches with 135, three with 155, and then six to eight sets of two repetition snatches with 180 pounds.

Most squat style snatchers will find a greater difference between their best single effort and the weight they can handle for repetitions than will the splitters.

The flip snatch, pulling the weight all the way up, is a good way to develop follow-through pull, even after split or squat technique has been mastered. The vital part of the pull is from the knees to the highest possible point, so an attempt should be made to develop explosive acceleration through this area. Pulling a weight heavier than the lifter's best snatch from knee to chest height, keeping elbows high, and not trying to turn over the hands, will help develop power. Practicing actual snatches from the top of the thighs, or from the knees, or lifting from knee-high boxes, will also develop the all-important second pull and finishing power. Other pulling power exercises will be discussed after the portion dealing with the clean and jerk. Assistance exercises should be done in sets of three repetitions, working to as much weight as can be handled.

The two-arms clean and jerk

The final of the three Olympic weight lifting tests is the one in which world champion athletes lift double their weight in the smaller classes and over 400 pounds in the heavyweight division. It is a test of great strength, explosive power, coordination, and —to a certain extent—stamina.

Rules for the lift state the barbell must be lifted in two distinct motions, one to the chest and a second overhead. Once overhead, the weight must be held under control for two seconds, until the referee signals that it may be lowered. Any amount of splitting or squatting to get under the weight is allowed in both clean and jerk, with the exception that a knee touch is forbidden in the clean (and jerk, for that matter, though there is seldom any danger of going that low in the second portion of the lift).

According to the rules, the first pull from the floor must place the barbell in the position at the shoulders from which it is to be lifted (jerked) overhead. The second part of the lift must be a single drive from the shoulders to locked arms overhead. If the

first jerk overhead is not held for the count, it may not be repeated a second time from the shoulders, and a second jerk overhead is also forbidden if the first one is successful. This latter
technicality is to prevent exhibitionism on the part of men who
seek to be spectacular by lifting heavy poundages overhead two
or more repetitions.

A strong pull is vital for the clean, especially the "second
pull" area from the knees to the highest possible point (where
the lifter catches the weight at the shoulders by squatting or
splitting). First the split style: The starting position is with feet
comfortably spaced and the barbell close to the shins. The lifter
grasps it with palms toward the legs, again using a comfortable
grip which is usually slightly wider than the shoulders. The pull
is started with the back flat, hips low, and head up. The initial
pull comes from the legs and back, with the vicious follow-
through of the arms whipping the barbell over to catch it at the
chest with elbows forward.

In the split style of lifting, (*See* Figure 53.) the weight is
started as described, with an easy starting pull, arms hanging
straight but not locked, and then pulled in close as it is accelerated to all the speed possible by pulling with the arms, thrusting
the hips forward, and rising quickly on toes at the height of the
pull. The rise-on-toes is continued into a front and back split
under the barbell as the hands are whipped over and the elbows
thrust forward. The correct position in catching the weight is
with the hips at least as low as the front knee, the front knee
ahead of the ankle, the body erect with the weight at the shoulders, the elbows forward to hold the weight at the chest, and
the rear leg placed solidly back and held under tension enough
not to be driven to the floor by the weight striking the chest.
When the weight is firmly in position at the chest, the lifter
straightens both legs simultaneously and then steps forward to
bring the feet on a line preparatory to jerking the barbell overhead.

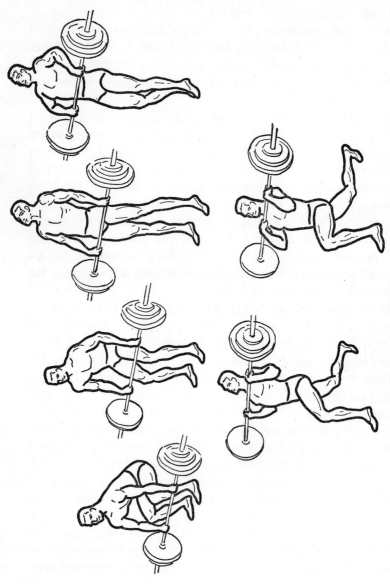

Figure 53. Two arms clean to shoulders (split style).

In the squat style of cleaning, (*See* Figure 54.) the initial pull is the same, started with legs and back from the flat-backed, head-up, hips-low position. The importance of pulling all out from knee height, thrusting the hips forward, and rising sharply on toes as the weight is pulled close cannot be over-emphasized. As the weight reaches the absolute height of possible pull, the lifter whips his hands over and his elbows well forward and up. At the same time, he jumps his feet apart (kicking off from the rise-on-toes) and squats to catch the weight at the chest. Theoretically the lifter's limit clean will be caught at the chest as he reaches the full squat, but with lesser weights, the barbell will be caught at the chest before the full squat is reached, after which the lifter will "hit bottom" and then rebound to rise and get set for the jerk. The correct low position is with the feet comfortably spread, toes turned out, the body erect, and elbows held high and forward. The clean may be disqualified if the officials detect the elbows coming in contact with the knees. Having the elbows strike the knees and the barbell strike the chest at the same time can also cause a painful strain to one or both wrists. For these two reasons, it is important to learn to get the elbows well forward and up. When the weight is solidly at the chest and balance is secure, the lifter drives strongly upward with both legs, keeping his feet firmly planted and elbows consciously held forward. In rising, the body should remain erect and the hips thrust forward under the weight as soon as possible. In most cases, the lifter will have placed his feet wider in cleaning than he will want them while driving to start the jerk, so they should be brought to what experience has shown to be the best jerking stance, as soon as the lifter has fully risen from the squat clean.

During the first part of the cleaning pull from the floor to knee height, there should be no deliberate attempt to pull slowly, but it is important that the lifter consciously try to accelerate the upward motion from knee height upward. It is also important that this "second pull" be continued to the last possible split second before the feet leave the floor to get under the weight. Too

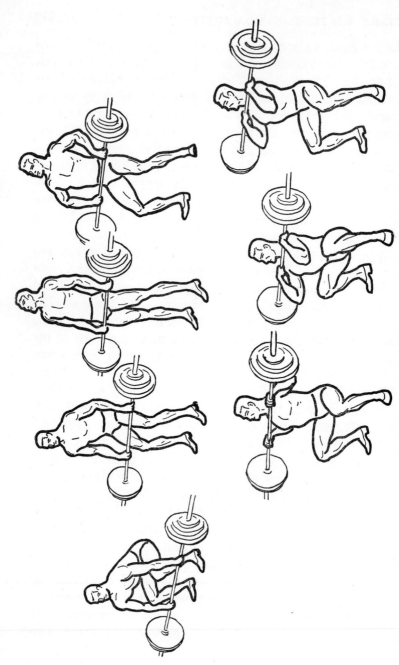

Figure 54. Two arms clean to shoulders (squat style).

many lifters fail to take full advantage of their pull by trying to split or squat under the weight too soon. Bob Hoffman has often said that a clean need only be pulled "six inches higher than a dead lift" for an efficient lifter to catch the weight at the chest in the deep split position. In practice, lifters often drop this low or lower, especially in the squat style, but are actually driven down after catching the weight higher. The weight must be pulled above belt height for even the fastest-moving athletes to get under it before it starts back toward the floor.

In writing about the split clean, Hoffman said, "Stand as close to the bar as you can without touching it . . . Wrap the thumb around the bar and then wrap the fingers around the bar, also encircling the thumb (hook grip) . . . To secure the grip on the bar the buttocks should be lowered as though you were going to sit slowly upon a very low chair . . . Now you are ready to . . . (start) the lift. The arms remain straight like ropes with hooks on the ends. They do not come into action until the weight has passed the knees. You are concentrating on pulling the weight straight up, keeping it as close to the body as possible . . . (still quoting Hoffman). The movement is relatively slow until the weight passes the knees. At this point every ounce of strength your body possesses should be exerted. Much of the final effort is done with a great exertion of the arms and shoulders . . . As the weight nears the chest the movement is so fast you can hardly see what takes place. You have pulled the weight as high as you can. At this point the champion is raised on toes with chest up and head back. Suddenly you lower the body under the weight. In splitting one foot goes to the front and the other to the rear. The distance should be about equal. At the same time the elbows are whipped suddenly upward and forward. The upper body is held erect, the back in, and the weight is placed on the upper chest. Most of the body's weight is placed on the front foot, which is held in the position of a one-legged squat, the knee in front of the foot, so that a further dip is possible if the weight is a bit forward ... From the low split come erect by bringing back the front leg."

Al Murray's instruction for the split clean is as follows: "(Get set with) feet ... astride, insteps under the bar, back flat, shoulder slightly in advance of the bar, head up, and eyes looking forward. Arms straight but not tensed. Hands slightly wider than shoulder breadth. Lead the pull with the head, shoulders, and hips at the same time, keeping the total weight evenly over the whole area of both feet. As the bar passes the knees thrust the hip upwards and forwards, lift the chest high, at the same time pulling hard vertically with the arms and shoulders. Concentrate on reaching your highest height on the ball(s) of both feet. Concentrate on both feet leaving the floor at exactly the same split second, so that you land in a balanced position beneath the bar."

Murray emphasizes the importance of the second pull, "As the bar passes the knees ... *the hips must be thrust viciously forwards and upwards towards the bar*. At the same time the chest is raised high to get the best results from the powerful extensors of hips and back ... (and) you must continue pulling fiercely ... with the arms."

Once the weight is firmly at the chest, Murray says, "Push upwards and backwards with the front leg using the rear leg as a straight-legged prop. The weight ... will be transferred over the rear foot, thus allowing you to recover the front foot a few inches backwards ... To complete the recovery lift the chest ... upwards pushing forwards with the rear leg which will bring the weight of the body and bar over the front foot, allowing you to bring both feet in line for the second part of the lift."

Harry Paschall says of the clean, "In this lift, as in the snatch, I am convinced that the squat method is the most efficient. You do not have to pull a weight so high to clean it by this technique ... You approach the bar, relaxed, stoop with flat back and hook both hands a bit wider than the shoulders. Flatten the back and pull easily until the bar reaches the knees—then, as in the snatch, *give it the works!* Pull hard up and back— go clear up on your toes and *keep pulling!* When you feel the end of the pull, do the same thing as in the snatch, *jump down* . . . under the barbell, whipping up the elbows to slap the bar into the shoulders. When it hits the deltoids, keep the elbows purposely lifted, as *high* as you can . . . (You) hit bottom on the squat, back straight, and heave with your hips to take advantage of the rebound at the bottom. You come up just as in the deep-knee-bend."

Note that Paschall mentions pulling back, while Murray and Hoffman do not. Murray says the weight should actually be farther forward when caught at the chest than when it leaves the floor. Hoffman says the weight should be pulled straight up. It seems certain that there will be some forward and then back, or some backward motion in the upward movement of the barbell, even if it is caught at the chest directly above its starting point. This would come from a natural action of the body in exerting all-out pull. In actual practice, most splitters move the rear foot farther back than the front foot goes forward. In cleaning weights of 400 pounds and more, Norbert Schemansky jumped both feet off the platform, but pulled back so strongly that the front foot returned to its starting point while the rear foot moved far back. Dave Sheppard, who cleaned 400 pounds while weighing 190, said he lifted in an S-curve, and in the clean, did appear to swing the weight out slightly at the height of the hips (after a pull in at the knees) and then finished by pulling back at the end of the clean, jumping back slightly as he squatted to catch the weight at the chest. Dr. McCloy refers to physics formulae in saying it is quite possible a pull-back might be more efficient, since a gradual rise involves less work than one straight up. McCloy says the pull-back could theoretically be stronger because in doing so the lifter would be able to make greater use of his own weight to lead the barbell. That is, the lifter's bodyweight would be moving slightly ahead of the barbell as it was pulled up and back. With individual differences in length of bones, and in point of muscle insertion, thus differing leverages, it seems possible that all the instructors may be right in individual cases. Important basic fundamentals:

THE CLEAN, SUMMARY

1. The weight must be pulled close to the legs and body.
2. The barbell should be accelerated upward from knee height.
3. Pull should be complete, with a follow-through to the full rise-on-toes that is completed by jumping with all the speed possible into the squat or split position.

Once the weight is at the chest, and the lifter has recovered from the split or squat position, the jerk overhead (*See* Figure 55.) is a simpler portion of the two-part lift. Sometimes it is made difficult by the fact that the lifter has expended too much energy in the clean, and lacks the stamina to drive the barbell successfully overhead. The start of the jerk is made with the feet placed comfortably on a line, separated to the distance from which the lifter has found he can drive upward best. The barbell should be held at the clavicle, resting on the shoulders, with elbows forward and body erect. To thrust the weight overhead, a short, quick dip of the knees and rebound is employed, and the feet are split front and back at the height of the drive. The arms are straightened forcibly to add their strength to the leg drive, and the lifter shifts his body forward so that the weight is caught directly over the head as he splits only low enough to catch the weight at the top of the thrust from the combined leg and arm drive. Lifters who use the split and squat styles in snatching and cleaning, all split to get under weights jerked overhead. With the weight overhead, the lifter straightens both legs and steps forward to bring the feet on a line and to hold the barbell until he receives the referee's signal that it may be lowered.

The important thing to remember in jerking is that the barbell must not be allowed to slide down on the chest as the leg drive is started by bending the knees. The elbows must be held forward of the barbell and the trunk erect so that the power delivered by

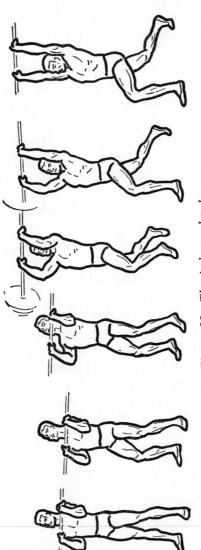

Figure 55. The jerk overhead.

the legs will be transferred directly to the upward movement of the barbell. There will be a power loss if the weight is allowed to move downward on the chest while the legs are driving upward.

Allowing the chest to slump and the elbows to move back of the barbell will also cause the weight to be jerked forward to a point where even a strong lifter cannot hold it overhead by arm and shoulder strength. A strong man can often remain momentarily in the split position and force the barbell to locked arms for a distance of several inches, in instances when the coordinated leg-arm drive has failed to send it all the way up. He will not be able to do so, however, if he has to bring the weight back to a point where he can control it and push upward at the same time.

Writing about jerking overhead, Hoffman says, "(P)lace the feet a comfortable distance apart. Hold the back straight and the head high; dip just a little and drive hard, then split under the weight. It's ridiculously easy."

After completing the clean, Harry Paschall says, "Here is the middle point of the clean and jerk, and the place where many lifters make their big mistake. They do not take time to get properly set to make the jerk, and either shoot up the weight while still off balance, or wait so long that they become exhausted. Actually you should get a brief period of rest at this point, a time to gather your energies for the final explosive effort that carries the bell to arms' length. Be sure the weight is well back on the raised deltoids, . . . then lift the elbows high, get the whole body set straight and strong with feet in line. Then breathe in, make a strong but controlled dip (not too far), and drive strongly upward, trying to send the weight up in a slightly backward direction over head . . . As the bar goes up, step firmly forward, dipping enough so that you drop beneath the bar with arms locked."

Al Murray describes the jerk as follows: "The get-set position for the jerk must be a well-balanced position with the elbows held forwards to secure the bar on the chest and the total weight equally distributed over both feet, forearms nearly vertical. The dip is a shallow, snappy knee bend and stretch to send the bar vertically upwards. Dip snappily ... (and) Rebound immediately ... by vigorously straightening both legs. Thrust the trunk upwards and forwards whilst keeping it in a vertical position throughout. Drive upwards viciously with both arms. This should bring you on the ball(s) of both feet. At this point, as in the fully extended position at the finish of the pull for the Snatch and Clean, *you leap off both feet, making sure once more that both feet leave the floor at exactly the same split second.* As the bar flies aloft, keep the chest high, and aim to place the upper arms vertically above the shoulder joints and behind the ears."

In training sessions, most lifters will find it profitable to spend most of their time devoted to the third lift, working on the clean to the chest. A workable percentage schedule is as follows:

Monday:

Having already been pulling and dropping low in the snatch, little special warm-up is needed for the clean. A few cleans without moving the feet and with slight dip, and then a few squats or splits with a light weight at the chest, and the lifter is ready to clean 70 per cent of limit three repetitions (lowering the barbell to the knees or below for repetitions); 75 per cent three repetitions; 80 per cent three repetitions; 85 to 90 per cent five to ten single cleans and jerks.

Wednesday:

Warm up and then clean 75 per cent of limit three repetitions; 80 per cent three repetitions; 85 per cent three single cleans; 90 to 95 per cent five or six single cleans and jerks.

Friday (or Saturday):

Warm up and then clean 75 per cent of limit three repetitions; 85 per cent three repetitions; 90 per cent two repetitions; 95 to 102½ per cent three single cleans and jerks.

For the majority of lifters, the jerk will be practiced sufficiently by completing a few heavy single lifts. A man who has trouble holding his jerks for one reason or another, however, should set aside one training day of the week for the practice of double jerks from the shoulders. He should start at about 70 per cent of limit and work up in 10-pound weight increases until he is unable to complete the second jerk. If this does not provide enough practice, he should then drop back to 70 per cent again for three to five sets of two jerks, depending on his reserve of energy.

Occasionally a poor arm lock will handicap a man in holding heavy weights overhead. In this case, a slightly wider grip will often help.

Other practical methods of training on the third lift are as follows:

Heavy Singles, Based on Best Clean and Jerk of 250 Pounds:

Clean 200 three repetitions, 220 three repetitions, and 235 or 240 five single cleans. Then five complete cleans and jerks with the same weight.

Heavy Doubles, Based on Best Clean and Jerk of 250 Pounds:

Clean 200 three repetitions, 220 three repetitions, and clean 230 six sets of two. Then clean 230 five or six more sets of two, jerking the weight overhead after the second clean.

Building power and strength

To develop pulling power and all-around body strength, which will aid in all three lifts, especially the snatch and clean, there are a number of good assistance exercises. There are five basic movements used by weight lifters the world over, and a number of variations. The basic five are: the squat, the high dead lift (also known as "power pulls"), the "power clean" (a clean without moving the feet), the supine press on bench, and the press with two dumbbells (described previously).

The power clean is an excellent movement to develop an all-out high pull. Power cleans are done as though to clean for the press without foot movement, and are repeated in sets of three repetitions. A lifter should start with about 10 or 20 pounds less than he can press and work up in 10-pound jumps as high as he can go with three repetitions. Occasionally it is a good idea to keep working up in 10- and 5-pound jumps to a limit single power clean.

Full squats are performed as described in the chapter dealing with basic exercise, but in sets of five and three repetitions for a total of approximately twenty squats. There are innumerable ways of working squats into a training program. One is to perform five with a weight approximately equal to the lifter's best clean and jerk; five more with an additional 20 pounds, then two more sets of five or three with 10-pound weight increases. Another system is simply to do four sets of five repetitions, or five or six sets of three repetitions with a weight heavier than the lifter's best clean.

Lifters using the squat style clean should perform knee bends with the weight at the chest, starting lower than their best clean, and working up to a single squat or repetitions with more than they can clean. Then, if additional strength work is desired, more weight can be added for a set or two of squats with the barbell behind the neck.

A variation of the squatting movement, which builds great ligament and tendon strength, is to take a weight much heavier than the lifter's best full squat and perform quick partial bends with the weight held at the chest. This can be repeated with even more weight held behind the head, but with the weight held at the chest, it will also help build strength for the jerk. A lifter able to squat with 300 pounds should do this exercise with 350–400 pounds.

The high dead lift pulling exercise is done like the beginning of a clean, but without attempting to drop and catch the weight. The barbell is grasped with buttocks low, back straight, and head up, and pulled steadily to the knees; at this point it is accelerated and pulled to touch the body as high as possible. (*See* Figure 56.) When the weight gets so heavy it cannot be pulled to the height of the belt, the exercise is beginning to lose some of its transfer value. This pulling movement should be done in sets of three repetitions, working up from a weight equal to the lifter's best clean to as heavy a weight as possible.

Figure 56. High dead lift.

Al Murray suggests several assistance exercises, which are excellent power builders, one of which is cleaning heavy dumbbells to the chest in sets of three or singles. This is a pulling-power movement that would be used to supplement a regular three-lift workout. As an assistance movement for the jerk, Murray recommends jerking weights overhead without moving the feet. This is another three-repetition movement that can be done in sets, working up from the weight of the lifter's best press. To build strength in the low split position, Murray advises lowering and raising the body with the legs in the fore-and-aft position. He describes the exercise as follows: "Assume (the split clean position) with the bar at the chest . . . Straighten both legs. You are now in the starting position. Lower by pushing the front knee forward and bending it at the same time you lower the body, so that the hip corresponding to the front leg is almost touching the front heel. Later when you are familiar with this exercise you should lower fairly quickly and rebound out of the low position. It is better to keep the weight light enough to perform three sets of six or eight repetitions." Murray suggests this exercise be done in conjunction with front squats, in order to build up both legs.

Arranging training schedules

With the great variety of exercises and variations available, it is a problem for the individual lifter or coach to arrange an efficient training schedule. Ideally, the schedule should allow ample time for practice of lifting technique, specializing on the individual's weaknesses and a variety of assistance exercises to develop needed power. The time available for training is also a factor, since it is necessary to rest three to five minutes after strenuous efforts.

For an average workout, based on the percentage increases for the three lifts, a program could be set up as follows:

1. Press—Total of eighteen presses, counting all sets from 70 per cent of limit.
2. Snatch—Total of fifteen-eighteen snatches.
3. Clean (and jerk)—Total of fifteen-eighteen cleans.
   (And five to ten jerks.)
4. Squat—Total of fifteen-twenty-five, in sets of five or five and three.
5. Supine press—Total of fifteen-eighteen in sets of three (or five and three).

If follow-through is needed in the pull, some of the snatches can be done flip style in a variety of ways: two sets of three flips before beginning to split or squat, or one or two flip snatches with a third in split or squat style in each set until the weight gets too heavy to pull all the way up. During one workout of the week, all the snatches can be performed flip style, though it will be necessary to handle less weight.

For additional pulling exercise, power cleans can be substituted for some of the split or squat cleans in the same manner. For still more pull, the high dead lift exercise can be substituted for the squats (total of fifteen-eighteen repetitions in sets of three) or three sets of squats and three sets of pulls could be used in the same workout.

Another method of breaking up the routine would be to practice the basic workout on Monday, perhaps using both squats and high dead lifts. Then on Wednesday, the flip snatches and power cleans could be included with the regular squatting routine, and on Friday (or Saturday) the power pulls could be substituted for squats, after practicing limit lifting.

Some lifters find they expend too much energy by working on heavy cleans and snatches the same day. In this case, experienced men press and snatch one day (plus auxiliary exercises) and press and clean the next, working all three lifts on limit days with fewer repetitions.

While retaining the competitive lifts as a basic program, plus one or two assistance exercises, there is an endless variety of training schedules possible that can be worked out to individual preference and needs. As the date of an actual competition nears, however, it is wise to practice the technique of lifting intensively, with less emphasis on variations and strength-building exercises. The week before a contest to be held on a Saturday, a final limit lifting day should be planned as a try-out. Then working up to the planned starting poundages can be included the Monday prior to the contest. On Wednesday, most lifters will find it will help to build a reserve of nervous energy not to work as high as the starting weights. Instead, they should take poundages they can handle easily and make a number of single lifts in as perfect style as possible. This tapering off, plus two days of rest before the contest, will enable the lifter to gain full strength after the heavy exercise he has been practicing, and will also bring him to a proper mental state of wanting to try for new personal records on all three lifts.

Selecting lifts in competition

Depending on the lifts taken by his competitors, a good practice is for the lifter to judge his condition in the warm-up room. He must, however, be careful not to overwork. If feeling fully up to standard, he can start with 10 or 15 pounds below his personal record in each lift. If the lift goes easily and he is not in close competition with another lifter, he can attempt to equal his personal best on his second attempt. If successful, he then has a third attempt in which to try 5 or 10 pounds more than he has lifted previously. If the second attempt is a failure, he has the option of repeating with the same weight.

The lifting by the opposition has considerable bearing on the choice of poundage. Most experienced lifters can accurately gauge what they will press on a given day. Few men press more in competition than in training, so the lifter can count on making about the same press as he did on his try-out day, though his two-day rest may have added enough to his strength to exceed it. At any rate, if the competition is close after the press, the lifter will want to stay with his opponent, or go ahead of him, in the snatch. An official will call off the weights until he reaches a poundage at which the lifter wants to make an attempt, so it is possible to keep a close watch on the competition.

A nervous type of individual can often rise to unexpected heights in the quick lifts, in which most men are able to lift more weight in competition than in training. Since the same type is often a comparatively poor presser, he has his chance to catch up on the second lift. After succeeding in a first attempt that is below his personal best, a highly competitive lifter, under pressure, can occasionally break his own record twice on successive lifts. Men have often lifted 10 to 20 pounds more in the snatch and clean and jerk than ever before, under the stimulus of competition.

In weight lifting, the clean and jerk is the "pay-off," so to speak, in which the final outcome of the contest is decided in each bodyweight class. Because heavy poundages are involved, because the competitors are becoming tired, and because men react differently to pressure, it is possible to overcome apparently insurmountable deficits in the final lift. A man who is ahead should be able to judge his opponents' strength by their performance on the first two lifts, and should attempt to make three successful lifts that will put his total out of reach. His opponents, on the other hand, must get in a "safe" lift to be among the place-winners, but must try enough to make up the difference in total on the third attempt. In some cases, it is wise to save two attempts until the leader has finished, in order to have two tries at the "all-or-nothing" poundage.

A lifter must be aware of the body weights of his closest competitors in order to take advantage of the rule that states the lighter man wins in case of a tie on total. An example of this was seen in the 1954 world championships. Dave Sheppard, 14 pounds lighter in the middleheavyweight class than his Russian opponent Vorobyev, made a first-attempt clean and jerk that ensured his placing no lower than second. Then he waited until Vorobyev made his final clean and jerk of 385 pounds. Both men had snatched 314 pounds, but Vorobyev had pressed the same weight, as compared with Sheppard's 286. To make up the 28-pound deficit, Sheppard would have had to break the world record clean and jerk in the class by 14 pounds, and he made two tries which kept Vorobyev's gold medal in jeopardy until the last second. Sheppard caught 413 pounds at the chest twice in the clean, but was unable to rise and complete the jerk. While he failed in this attempt to tie and win as lighter man, it does illustrate the great poundages a lifter can attempt in an effort to win. In this case Sheppard came close to success in the apparently impossible. Others have succeeded in similar cases.

Although, in the preceding discussion, Sheppard was far too light in his class so that his strength suffered, it is a good idea to weigh in as lighter man when close competition is expected.

Making weight by cutting foods that are fattening, and by almost eliminating liquids, is well known. Additional ounces can be removed at the last minute by chewing gum and expectorating saliva. Extreme methods of reducing, such as the steam room, are not recommended for lifters because they may unduly weaken the competitor. It is far better for a man to compete at a weight that he knows will find him strong and quick.

Making weight, to the extent that it does not reach a point of diminishing returns in strength as opposed to the strength of competitors, does have its place in weight lifting. This is especially true in important championships. Occasionally a natural middleweight will be able to reduce to the lightweight class and still beat his competitors, even though he cannot lift as well as at his normal weight. It also happens on occasion that an unusually strong man is competing in a medium weight class, in which case, an almost-as-strong opponent may find less opposition in the class above! Filling up on water and food immediately before the weigh-in will usually take care of going a few ounces over the class limit.

The following is a list of some of the outstanding official totals lifted by competitors the world over:

Bantamweight Class (123): Stogov (Russia) 738; Udodov (Russia) 705¼; Namdjou (Iran) 699; Charles Vinci (U.S.A.) 699; Farkhutdinov (Russia) 694; Vilkhovski (Russia) 694; Chalfin (Russia) 682; Korsh (Russia) 682; Joseph DePietro (U.S.A.) 677½.

Featherweight Class (132): Udodov (Russia) 782; Chimishkyan (Russia) 771; Saxonov (Russia) 748; Chavez (Panama) 742¾; Fayad (Egypt) 732; Tun Maung (Burma) 727; Mazurenko (Russia) 721½; Mahgoub (Egypt) 721½; Yas Kuzuhara (U.S.A.) 720; Wilkes (Trinidad) 716; Anderson (Sweden) 716; Mannironi (Italy) 716.

Lightweight Class (148): Kostylev (Russia) 843; Tommy Kono (U.S.A.) 832; Ivanov (Russia) 826; Falamejev (Russia) 826; Tony Terlazzo (U.S.A.) 825; Pete George (U.S.A.) 815; Sheglov (Russia) 815; Stan Stanczyk (U.S.A.) 810; Nikitin (Russia) 810; Gouda (Egypt) 804½.

Middleweight Class (165): Kono (U.S.A.) 931¼; Duganov (Russia) 898; Bogdanovsky (Russia) 898; Stanczyk (U.S.A.) 892; George (U.S.A.) 892; Touni (Egypt) 881; Novak (Russia) 881; Dave Sheppard

(U.S.A.) 876; Yagli-Ogli (Russia) 865; Frank Spellman (U.S.A.) 859; Gerald Gratton (Canada) 859.

Lightheavyweight Class (181): Kono (U.S.A.) 966½; Novak (Russia) 953¼; Lomakin (Russia) 953¼; Vorobyev (Russia) 947½; Sheppard (U.S.A.) 937; Stepanov (Russia) 936¾; Stanczyk (U.S.A.) 931.

Middleheavyweight Class (198): Vorobyev (Russia) 1014¼; Sheppard (U.S.A.) 1008½; Osipa (Russia) 986¾; Norbert Schemansky (U.S.A.) 980½; Lomakin (Russia) 953¼; Clyde Emrich (U.S.A.) 950; Bulgakov (Russia) 909¼.

Heavyweight Class (over 198): Paul Anderson (U.S.A.) 1146½; Schemansky (U.S.A.) 1074¼; John Davis (U.S.A.) 1062½; Jim Bradford (U.S.A.) 1047; Doug Hepburn (Canada) 1040; Medvedev (Russia) 1008½; Selvetti (Argentina) 1008½; Steve Stanko (U.S.A.) 1002; Dave Baillie (Canada) 1000.

Outstanding Individual Lifts, Press: 123: Stogov, 235¾—DePietro, 231—Kirshon, 225¼—Farkhutdinov, 220¼; *132:* Udodov, 245—Kirshon, 244½—DelRosario, 239¾—Khanushvili, 236¼—DePietro, 234½—Nam, 231—Bob Higgins, 231—Chavez, 231; *148:* Nikitin, 264½—Ivanov, 259—Terlazzo, 255—Nicholls, 255; *165:* Kono, 292—Alex Pilin, 287½—Novak, 285½—Touni, 281—Bogdanovsky, 281; *181:* Kono, 316¼—Novak, 315¼—Lomakin, 303; *198:* Vorobyev, 319½—Osipa, 317¼—Novak, 316¼—Sheppard, 308½—Emrich, 300—Bloomberg, 300; *Heavyweight:* Anderson, 409—Hepburn, 381—Bradford, 363¾—Selvetti, 352½—Davis, 342.

Outstanding Individual Lifts, Snatch: 123: Vinci, 225¾—Vilkhovski, 220½—Stogov, 220¼—Udodov, 216—Namdjou, 215—Mahgoub, 214¾; *132:* Chimishkyan, 242½—Saxonov, 238¼—Fayad, 231—Udodov, 231; *148:* Kostylev, 271—Gouda, 262—Kono, 259—Sheglov, 259—Shams, 256¾—Sheppard 252; *165:* Duganov, 292—George, 281—Sheppard, 281—Kono, 280; *181:* Sheppard, 303¼—Vorobyev, 299¾—Stanczyk, 292—Novak, 288—Lomakin, 286½—Stepanov, 286½; *198:* Sheppard, 316½—Vorobyev, 314¼—Schemansky, 308½—Osipa, 308½; *Heavyweight:* Schemansky, 334—Davis, 330½—Bradford, 320—Anderson, 320—Stanko, 310½—Herb Schiff, 310—Medvedev, 308½—Louis Abele, 300—Baillie, 300.

Outstanding Individual Lifts, Clean and Jerk: 123: Stogov, 286½—Yu In Ho, 285—Namdjou, 282—Udodov, 281; *132:* Chimishkyan, 315¼—Saxonov, 313—Fayad, 303—Udodov, 303; *148:* Shams, 338¾—Terlazzo, 331—George, 330½—Falamejev, 330½—Gouda, 330½; *165:* Kono, 371¼—George, 364½—Bogdanovsky, 352¼—Duganov, 349½; *181:* Lomakin, 381¼—Kono, 380¼—Vorobyev, 374¾—Ferrari, 372¾—Sheppard, 370; *198:* Schemansky, 399—Vorobyev, 391¼—Sheppard, 391¼—Emrich, 380; *Heavyweight:* Anderson, 436½—Schemansky, 425—Davis, 402—Medvedev, 391¼.

TABLE 8

Official Records (Total) Established During International Competition
(Three or more nations in contest.)

	Press	Snatch	C&J	Total	Date
N. Stogov (Russia) 123	231¼	220¼	286½	738	10-13-55
R. Chimishkyan (Russia) 132	231¼	236¾	303	771	10-7-54
I. Udodov (Russia) 132	236¾	231¼	303	771	10-7-54
N. Kostylev (Russia) 148	248	275½	319½	843	10-14-55
T. Kono (U.S.A.) 165	286½	264½	352½	903½	10-17-54
Kono, 165	264½	264½	369¼	898¼	8-29-53
Kono, 181	314¼	275½	374¾	964½	3-15-55
A. Vorobyev (Russia) 198	314¼	314¼	385¾	1014¼	10-10-54
P. Anderson (U.S.A.) hvy	407¾	319½	402¼	1129½	10-17-55

As will be noted from a comparison of the above with the outstanding individual totals listed previously, in many cases the official marks are lower than the "outstanding" ones. This is because of a technicality in the rules of the International Weight Lifting Federation, which accepts individual lift records made anywhere, any time under official conditions, but which accepts world record totals only when they are lifted during international competition (defined as contests involving three or more nations). The authors cannot understand the reasoning behind this rule, since in many instances press, snatch, and clean and jerk records are accepted as world standards while the total to which they added is ignored.

This was the case several times when Paul Anderson broke both press, and clean and jerk records, but did not receive official recognition for the fact that at the same time he scored totals more than 60 pounds higher than anyone else had lifted. In successive meets, Anderson lifted 402-315-425¼ for 1142¼, 403½-300-434 for 1137½, and 390-320-436½ for 1146½.

Udodov's best total was made during competition in Russia, and Kono's best middleweight total was made during a U.S. versus the Soviet Union team contest.

References

(1) BOOKS

   (1) Barnholth, Lawrence, *Secrets of the Squat Snatch.* Akron, Ohio: The American College of Modern Weight Lifting, 1950.
   (2) Hoffman, Bob, *Guide to Weight Lifting Competition.* York, Pa.: Strength and Health Publishing Company, 1940.
   (3) Murray, Al, *Basic Weight Training.* London: George Grose Ltd.
   (4) ————, *The Theory and Practice of Olympic Lifting.* London: George Grose Ltd., 1954.
   (5) Murray, Jim, *Weight Lifting and Progressive Resistance Exercise.* New York: A. S. Barnes and Company, 1954.
   (6) Paschall, Harry B., *Bosco's Strength Notebook,* Vol. 1, No. 1. Alliance, Nebraska: Iron Man Publishing Company, 1951.
   (7) ————, *Bosco's Strength Notebook,* Vol. 1, No. 2. Alliance, Nebraska: Iron Man Publishing Company.
   (8) ————, *Development of Strength.* London: Vigour Press Ltd.

Index

AAU, 7, 14, 21, 157, 160–161
Abdominal muscles, strengthening of, 83,
    106, 111, 131, 138
Abele, Louis, 206
Age, weight lifting and, 31–33
Ameche, Alan, 115
American College of Modern Weight
    Lifting, 16, 178
Anderson, Paul, 6–8, 16–17, 20, 41–42,
    111–112, 167, 206–207
Apollo Health Studios, 38–39
Arizona, University of, 103
Arms, strengthening of, 38, 72, 75–77, 80,
    85–87, 97–98, 107–108, 128, 138, 149
Aronis, Alex, 115
Athletes, food for, 58–64
    (*See also* kind of athlete, as Baseball
    player)
Athletic clubs, 6, 17, 45, 65
Augustine, Jim, 18
Awkwardness, exercise to overcome, 125

Bachtell, Dick, 15
Back muscles, absolute strength of,
    40–41
    development of, 72, 77, 80–81, 89–91,
    97, 107–108, 138
    relative strength of, 40–41

Backus, Bob, 130, **137**
Bailey, Ed, 17
Baillie, Dave, 206
Baker, Bob, 144
Bantamweight class, 20, 160
    records set in, 205
Barbells, 4–10, 12, 23–24, 31, **36**, **48**,
    50–51, 72, 104–105, 158
    adjustable, 6
    basic exercises with, 75–83
    correct use of, 107–108
    graded, 13
    grip on, 163
    solid, nonrevolving, 11–12
    taping hands to, 66
    variation exercises with, 84–100, 119–
    120, 126, 129, 138, 140–141, 144
Barberis, 21
Barnes, Walter, 115
Barnholth, Larry, 178, 184, 208
Barnholth brothers, 16, 184
Baseball players, exercises for, 126–129
Basketball players, exercises for, 122–125
Bates Barbell Club, 16
Bent-arm lateral raise, 95–96
    lying, 82, 99, 147, 149
"Bent press" lift, 8
Berger, Al, **112**

Berry, Mark, 13
Blood pressure, weight lifting and, 56–58
Bloomberg, 206
Body, effect of weight lifting on, 51–66
Body building, 22–23, 72
Body measurements, weight training and, 38–39
Bogdanovsky, 20, 205
Bossio, Bill, 144
Boston Marathon, 59
Boxers, exercises for, 144–145
Bradford, Jim, 18–20, 206
Bread, 63
Bronze medals, 21
Brown, Elmer, 118
Bruce, George R., 153
Bulgakov, 206

Calories, energy and, 54
  number of, for athletes, 62–63
Calvert, Alan, 13, 24
Capen, E. K., 45, 66
Capillaries, 35
Carbohydrates, 62
Cereal, 63
Cerutty, Percy, 103
Chalfin, 205
Chandler, Otis, 130, 135, 153
Charite, 21
Chavez, Carlos, 21, 206
Chest, muscle development of, 72, 78, 81, 88–89
Chimishkyan, 19–20, 41–42, 205–207
Chinning, 137–138
Chui, E., 45, 66
Clean and jerk lift, 12, 16, 41–43, 49, 52, 131, 148
  individual records for, 206–207
  two-arms, 186–198
Cleans and cleaning, 107–108, 116, 123, 126, 131, 136–138, 141, 147, 149
Cleveland, Dick, 23, 141, 143
Climbing stairs, 125
  energy used in, 52–54
Clubs (see Athletic clubs)
Coaches, 103–111, 151, 167–168, 170, 181, 184
  basketball, 122–125
  football, 118–119
  swimming, 141, 143–144
Colleges, 46–47, 65, 103, 115, 160
Competition weight lifting, clothing worn in, 159
  equipment for, 158
  officials for, 158–159
  records set in, 205–207
  training for, 170–172, 185, 197
Cowles, Ozzie, 125
Cureton, T. K., 67
Curls and curling, 36, 75–76, 85–86, 93, 95–96, 98–99, 110, 112, 116, 123, 131, 133, 141, 143–144, 147
Cyr, Louis, 11–12

Davis, John, 15–19, 47–48, 112, 206
Dead lift, 80, 95–96, 99, 110–112, 144, 147
  high, 198–200
Delaitte, Albert, 24
De Lorme, Thomas L., 67
DelRosario, 21, 206
De Pietro, 16, 18, 205–206
Desbonnet, Edmund, 12
Diets, high protein, 60–61, 64
  for weight lifters, 61–64
Discus throwers, 136
Donelan, Paul F., 153
Drohan, John, 153
Duey, Henry, 15
Duganov, 205–206
Dumbbells, 4, 11–13, 23–24, 31, 72, 104–105
  basic exercises with, 75–83
  variation exercises with, 84–100, 126, 128, 138, 141, 144

Eder, Marvin, 111
Emrich, Clyde, 18, 20, 206
Endurance, 4
  training for, 37
Energy, in foods, 54, 58–59
  glycogen and, 35–36
  potential, 36
  used in weight lifting, 51–54
Ermolaiev, 57
Europe, 5–10, 13–14, 20, 158
Exercise, 4, 9, 17, 63
  courses of, 13, 22
  equipment for, 104–105
  group, 105–107
  to keep fit, 100, 128–129, 149–151
  planned, 48–49
  remedial, 117–118
  resistance (see Resistance exercise)
  for underweight, 98

Falamejev, 205
Farbotnek, John, 143
Farkhutdinov, 19, 42, 206
Fats, 62–63
Fayad, 20, 205–206
Featherweight class, 15, 20–21, 160
  records set in, 205
Feller, Bob, 126
Fencers, exercises for, 149
Ferguson, Fraysher, 38–39, 141, 143, 153
Ferrari, 206
Ferreira, 21
Findlay, Frank, 104
Fish, 61–63
Flexibility of muscles, 44, 47–48
Flowers, Keith, 118
Fonville, Charles, 135
Food, for athletes, 58–64
  energy and, 54, 58–59
  fried, 64
Foot weights, 93, 104, 125, 131, 133, 135

Football players, exercises for, 93, 98, 114–121
Fuchs, Jim, 135
Full squats, 17, 199

Gallagher, J. R., 67
Games, competitive, 4–5
Garth, Dick, 122
Gelatine, 59–60
George, Jim, 20, 42
George, Pete, 16, 18–20, 205–206
Glycogen, 35–36
Goellner, William, 153
Goerner, Herman, 7–8, 112
Gold medals, 19–20
Golfers, exercises for, 147–148
Good, Bill, 15
Gordien, Fortune, 23, 130, 136
Gouda, 205–206
Gratton, Gerald, 206
Grimek, John, 15, 21, 47–48
Grips, 11–12
Group exercises, 105–106

Hack lift, 91
Hack squat, 95
Hackenschmidt, George, 9–10, 24, 91, 94
Haller, 21
Hammer throwers, exercises for, 136
Heavyweight class, 6, 15–16, 20–21, 40, 160
   records set in, 206
Heidenstam, Oscar, 120, 153
Height, 20
Hepburn, Doug, 6, 19, 21, 24, 111, 166–167, 206
Hernias, 65
Higgins, Bob, 18, 206
High protein diet, 60–61
High schools, 65, 115
Hips, development of, 78, 90–91
Hoffman, Bob, 13–14, 18, 24, 47, 100, 104, 167, 180, 183, 191, 196, 208
Hopman, Harry, 103
Hurdlers, exercises for, 133

Injuries, from exercise, 72
   knee, 117–118, 125
   shoulder, 129
   in weight lifting, 64–66
Instructors, 103, 152
   grading by, 109–111
   points for emphasis by, 107–108
Intelligence, strength and, 30–31
International teams, 18
International Weight Lifting Federation, 207
Intestinal gas, foods causing, 63–64
Iowa, State University of, 24, 103, 122–123
Iowa State College, 44
Iron Man, 25, 65
Ishikawa, Emerick, 16

Ismayr, 21
Ivanov, 19, 42, 205–206

Javelin throwers, exercises for, 136–137
Jefferson lift, 92, 144
Jensen, Jackie, 129
Johnson, D. G., 120, 153
Jones, Art, 18
Jones, Stan, 115
Journal of Physical Education, 65
Jumpers, exercises for, 133, 135
Jumping, 123
   rope, 124–125

Karpovich, 31, 45, 47–48, 63, 65, 67
Keeney, 41, 43, 67
Kelly, Jack, Jr., 23, 146–147
Kettlebells, 8
Khanushvili, 206
Kilgour, Lennox, 20
Kim, 21
Kiner, Ralph, 126
Kintisch, I. L., 47, 67
Kirshon, 206
Knee bends, 12, 77–78, 92, 110, 112, 123–124, 133, 149
Knees, injured, remedial exercises for, 117–118, 125
Kono, Tommy, 16, 18–20, 41–42, 112, 167, 205–207
Korsh, 205
Kostylev, 20, 205, 205–207
Krestovnikoff, 41, 49, 53, 67
Kusinitz, I., 67
Kusuhara, Yas, 16, 18, 54, 205

Landy, John, 104
Lateral raise, 96, 127
   leaning, 87–88, 95
   lying, 82, 144, 149
   standing, 82–83, 95–96, 99, 123, 136, 143–144, 149
Leg curl, 93, 96, 99
Leg extensor exercise, 117–118, 125
Leggett, Leslie, 53
Leg-raises, 131, 133, 135, 138
Legs, development of, 72, 79–80, 93–94, 107–108, 119, 138
Leibsch, 21
Leight, Frank, 112–113
Lifts, energy used in, 51–54
   exercise, outstanding performances in, 111–113
   muscles used in, 52 n.
   records set in, 206–207
   used in competition, 157, 161–198
   selection of, 203–205
   (*See also* kind of lift, as Press)
Lightheavyweight class, 15, 18, 160
   records set in, 206
Lightweight class, 15, 160
   records set in, 205
Lomakin, 19, 206

McCloy, Charles H., 24, 48, 113, 120, 122–123, 128, 137, 153, 193
McCormick, W. J., 67
McCurdy, James H., 55, 67
Mahgoub, 206
Mail-order instructors, 12–15
Manger, 21
Mannironi, 205
Masley, J. W., 47, 67
Mats, 104
Maung, Tun, 21, 205
Mayor, Dave, 15, 112
Mazurenko, 205
Meat, 62–63
Medvedev, 206
Mental alertness, physical fitness and, 4
Mexico, 170
Middleheavyweight class, 160
　records set in, 206
Middleweight class, 15, 160
　records set in, 205–206
Milk, 61, 63
Milo Barbell Company, 13
Minerals, 59
"Mr. America" contests, 21–22, 45, 71, 112
　exercises for, 96–97
"Mr. Universe" contests, 21, 97
Mitchell, Bob, 15
Motor units, 35
Mueller, Edgar, 24
Murray, Al, 100, 168, 181–183, 192–193, 196, 200–201, 208
Murray, Jim, 100, 153, 208
Murray Cross, 182–183
Muscle-bound athletes, 45, 47–48
Muscle fiber, 34–35, 37
Muscle tone, exercise and, 72
Muscles, for baseball, 127
　for basketball, 124
　for boxing, 145
　composition of, 34–36
　efficient use of, 52–53
　energy expended by, 52–53
　for fencing, 150
　for field, 135
　flexibility of, 44
　for football, 116
　inflation of, 22
　rate of growth of, 37–39
　resistance exercise and, 72
　rest for, 48–50, 74
　for rowing, 146
　speed tests for, 45–46
　strength and, 34–50
　for swimming, 142
　for tennis and golf, 148
　for track, 134
　training of, 36–37, 72
　for wrestling, 140
　(See also parts of body, as Shoulders)
Muscular definition, 97
Musculature, diagrams of, 73

Nam, 206
Namdjou, Mahmoud, 20, 205–206
Narcissus complex, 29–30
National AAU Weight Lifting Championship Meet, 45
National Research Council, Food and Nutrition Board, 63
National YMCA Physical Education Council, 65
Neck, muscle development of, 94–95, 119
New York City, 45
Nicholls, 206
Nikitin, 205
Northern YMCA, Detroit, 16–17
Nosseir, El Saied, 20
Novak, Gregory, 18–19, 166–167, 205–206

Oarsmen, exercises for, 146–147
O'Brien, Parry, 23, 130
O'Connor, Frank (Bucky), 123–124
Ohio State University, 141, 143
Olympic Games, ancient Greek, 3–4
　modern, 7, 10, 13–16, 18–21, 41–43, 61, 130–132, 140–141, 144, 157, 170
One-hand snatch lift, 9–11, 49
Oshima, Niets, 18
Osipa, 206
Overhead lift, 9, 11
　(See also Press, overhead)

Park, Jim, 97–98, 112
Paschall, Harry B., 10, 24, 100, 168–169, 184, 192–193, 196, 208
Peoples, Bob, 112
Physical fitness, 4
　basic exercises for, 71–83
Pilin, Alex, 206
Pitkin, Professor, 30
Pitman, Joe, 16, 18
Pole vaulters, exercises for, 133–134
Popova, N. K., 67
Power, development of, 198–201
Power cleans, 198–199
Power pulls, 198
Press, 41–43, 49, 76–77, 96, 98–99, 108, 110, 116, 123, 126, 131, 133, 136–138, 141, 143, 147, 149, 164–165
　alternate, 124, 136–137, 143–144, 147, 152
　on bench, 81, 95, 99, 142–143
　on incline, 95, 99, 142
　individual records for, 206–207
　overhead, 119–120, 138, 140, 142
　supine, 98, 111, 116, 127, 133, 136–137, 141–145, 149, 198
　two-arm, 161–173
Proteins, 58, 60, 62
Pull to waist height, 54
Pullover, 95–96, 116, 127, 131, 133, 136–137, 141, 144, 147, 149–150
　bent-arm, 95
　straight-arm, 78–79

Pulse rate, weight lifting and, 55–56
Punching bags, 145

Research Quarterly, 46
Resistance exercises, 50
  for baseball players, 126–129
  basic conditioning and, 71–83
  for basketball players, 122–125
  for competitive lifters, 198–201
  for football players, 114–121
  for "minor" sports, 139–152
  for track and field, 130–138
  variations of, 84–100
Richards, Bob, 23, 130–132, 134
Rigoulot, Charles, 10, 16, 25, 112
Rise-on-toes, 79–80, 94–96, 99
Rope climbing, 131, 137
Rope skipping, 141, 145
Rowing, 77, 95–96, 98–99, 116, 140–141, 146–147
  upright, 80–81, 143
Rudd, J., 64, 67
Runners, exercises for, 133, 135
Running, 116, 141, 145
Ruptures, 64

Sakata, Harold, 18
Sandow, Eugene, 11–13
Sargent standing and running jump, 45
Saxon, Arthur (Hennig), 8–11, 25
Saxon brothers, 9–10
Saxonov, 19, 205
Schemansky, Norbert, 7–8, 16–19, 41–42, 183–184, 193, 206
Schemansky brothers, 17
Schiff, Herb, 206
Schleuter, Walter, 144
Sedgman, Frank, 104, 147
Selective Service Examination, 65
Selvetti, 21, 206
Shams, Ibrahim, 20, 206
Sheglov, 205
Sheppard, Dave, 16, 18, 180, 193, 205–206
Shot put, 45
Shot putters, exercises for, 136
Shoulder shrugging, 137
Shoulders, development of, 72, 76–77, 87–88, 97–98, 107–108, 119, 128, 137
  injured, exercise for, 129
Side bend, 93, 95, 99
Siebert, Theodore, 12
Sills, Frank, 122
Simonovich, Bill, 125
Sit-ups, 83, 95–96, 99, 111–113, 125, 127, 136–138, 141, 145, 147
Snatch lift, 41–43, 49
  individual records for, 206–207
  one-hand, 9–11, 49
  split, 56–57
  two-arm, 173–186
Speed, 10, 45–48
  test for, 45–46

Spellman, Frank, 16, 18, 206
Split snatch, 56–57
Sports, 4, 24
  (*See also* kind of sport, as Baseball)
Springfield College, 46–47, 53
Squats and squatting, 77–78, 91, 95–96, 98–99, 108, 116, 118–119, 123, 127, 132–133, 136–138, 141, 143–144, 147–150, 198–199
  one-legged, 132
Stance, 164
Stanczyk, Stan, 16, 18–19, 205–206
Stanko, Steve, 15–16, 167, 206
Steinbach, Josef, 6
Steinborn, Henry, 12, 112
Stepanov, 20, 206
"Sticking point," 73, 95
  working past, 74
Stogov, 20, 205–207
Stranahan, Frank, 23, 147
Strength, 3, 5, 125
  development of, 38, 198–201
  exercising for, 71–83, 134, 150–151
  muscles and, 34–50
  weight and, 40–44
Strength (magazine), 13
Strength and Health (magazine), 14, 25, 65
Strongmen, 20
  professional, 47
    American, 11–12
    European, 5–10
Sugar, 59
Sullivan award, 7
Super Strength, Calvert, 13
Sweets, 59
Swimmers, exercises for, 141–144
Swimming, 53
Swingbells, 84–86
Swoboda, Karl, 6–7, 24

Tendons, 37
Tennis players, exercises for, 147
Terlazzo, Tony, 15, 205–206
Terpak, John, 15, 18, 170
Terry, John, 15, 112
Tests, for speed and strength, 45
  for weight training classes, 109–111
Texas Christian University, 118
Thighs, development of, 78, 91–93, 131
Three-lift total, 16–17
Throwing practice, 127–128
"Thumbless grip," 163
Tom, Richard, 17–18
Tomita, Richard, 17
Touni, Khadr El, 20, 205–206
Town Club of Chicago, 143–144
Track and field, exercises for, 130–138
Training schedules, arranging of, 201–202
Travis, Warren Lincoln, 12
Trunk exercises for, 93
Turpin, Randy, 144
Tuttle, W. W., 44, 67

Twilight of the American Mind, The, Pitkin, 31
Two-arm snatch, 173–186
Two-arms clean and jerk, 186–198
"Two-hands anyhow" lift, 8

Udodov, 19–20, 205–207
Uhalde, Dan, 18
Underweight, exercises for, 98, 125
United States, 20–23
  competitive games in, 5, 139
  instructors in, 13, 103–104
  weight lifting in, 4, 10, 158, 160
U.S. championships, 15, 17, 21
U.S. teams, 14–15, 18

Van Buren, Steve, 115
Van Cleef, Ray, 104
Vegetables, 59, 63
Vilkhovski, 205–206
Vinci, Charles, 20, 111, 205–206
Vitamins, 59, 61, 64
Volley ball, 47
Vorobyev, 19–20, 42, 206–207

Wagner, 21
Walker, Ronald, 21
Warm-up before exercise, 75, 95–96, 98–99, 142
Weight, body, 6–7, 17, 20, 134
  energy used and, 54
  reduction in, 44
    through exercise, 74, 97
  strength and, 40–44, 111
Weight lifting, age and, 31–32
  brains and, 30–31
  competition, 157–208
  effects on body, 51–66
  equipment for, 158
  injuries in, 64
  international character of, 18–21, 61
  mechanical efficiency of, 53
  popularity of, 31
  rise of, in U.S., 4, 11–24
  without weights, 50, 138

Weight training, 22–23, 46
  age and, 32
  body measurements and, 38–39
  conditioning value of, 23–24
  courses in, 13, 22
  equipment for, 104–105
  exercises for (*see* Exercises)
  and other sports, 14, 48, 103–104, 114
Weight training classes, grading of, 109–111
Weighted sandals, 93, 104, 118
Weights, 6–9, 111
  for competition, 158
  early, 5
Wendler, Arthur, 122
Wheat germ oil, 61
Whitfield, Mal, 130, 132
Wiggins, Al, 143
Wilkes, Rodney, 20, 205
Wilkins, B. M., 47, 67
Willoughby, David P., 24
Wittenberg, Henry, 23, 140
Women, exercises for, 143–144
World championships, 14–18, 41–42, 170, 205–207
World heavyweight records, 21, 206–207
World War II, 15–16, 18, 60, 65
Wrestlers, exercises for, 139–141
Wrestler's bridge, 94, 116, 141, 145
Wrestling, 3, 5, 9–10, 47
Wrist curl, 85–86, 128
Wrists, strengthening of, 85–86, 128, 147

Yagli-Ogli, 206
Yarick, Ed, 16–18
York Barbell Company, 13, 23
York Oil Burner Athletic Club, 14–17
Yoshioka, George, 17
You, Richard, 17
YMCA, 13–14, 17, 65, 129
Yu In Ho, 206

Zagurski, Wally, 15
Ziegler, John B., 56–57
Zorbas, William S., 31, 45, 67